PUNK SNOT DEAD

MORAT

Thank you: Tempted as I am to put 'thanks to no fucker' because it looked good on a Discharge record, my gratitude is owed once more to Ulla Schrelle for her encouragement and hawk-eyed proofreading skills. I would also like to thank the many bands whose music was an inspiration. It would take an entire book to list them all, but the Damned, Sex Pistols, Siouxsie and the Banshees, Killing Joke, the Birthday Party, the Ruts, Stiff Little Fingers, Discharge, the Exploited, Dead Kennedys, Crass, UK Subs, and Motörhead all played a part in the writing of this book. If not for them I'd probably have a real job. Last but by no means least, I would like to thank my wife, Masuimi, a constant distraction without whom I would be lost. Love you, wifey.

Printed in the United States of America

First Printing, 2019

ISBN-13: 978-0-578-55015-2

Aberrant Publishing

ALSO BY THIS AUTHOR

THE ROAD TO FERO CITY

THE ROAD TO ROO INN

FOR SARAH AND ADAM

CHAPTER ONE

A FATIGUED AND battered-looking blue van pulled into the grass verge and sat sputtering and belching smoke into the summer dusk. It must have stopped to pick me up; no one in their right mind would risk stopping a wreck like that just to play the oh-so-hilarious game of driving away when I got close to the door. It might never build up enough speed to get away. After just over five hours of hitching – many of them spent reluctantly playing said game – it seemed that I finally had a ride, albeit one that moved no faster than walking pace.

The rear windows were filthy, impossible to see inside, so there was always the risk that the vehicle was full of drunken football thugs intent on pounding my face to mush, but there is a risk involved in taking any ride, every driver a potential rapist or serial killer. It's not like I was in any position to be choosy, particularly now that it was starting to get dark. Not that there was ever really much of a plan, but there sure as hell wasn't a Plan B.

Due as much to my own ignorance as a lack of luck with hitching, I was already running several hours later than anticipated. It's roughly seven and a half miles from the Strand in central London – where I had stopped to buy a ticket for tomorrow's Killing Joke show – to the start of the M1 motorway, and unaware that I could just get the tube up to Brent Cross – unaware that there even was a Brent Cross – I had walked all the way.

In my defence, I lived in a small village on the Isle of Wight, and although I'd been to London many times for gigs, I'd never tried to hitch from London to anywhere and had no idea of its vast scale. In fact, I'd never tried to hitch anywhere that wasn't on the island. Most of the time I'd taken the train up from Southampton, which conveniently plopped me out at Waterloo station, a short walk from the Lyceum where most of those gigs took place. And with bus services on the Isle of Wight being infrequent at best, I was also well accustomed to walking. It took an hour just to get to the ferry at Yarmouth.

With the benefit of hindsight and Google Maps, it seems rather foolish, to say the least, all the way up Southampton Row, up through Camden, Hampstead, and Golders Green, uphill all the way. But it was a pleasant walk, a hot summer's day, with no overtly dodgy neighbourhoods – at least not during daylight hours – and the simple joy of seeing new sights before they became familiar and mundane. By the end of the year I'd be living in a squat in Stoke Newington, a predominately Jewish area, but on that day Golders Green, another Jewish neighbourhood, was like another world. Suffice to say, you don't see many orthodox Jews growing up on the Isle of Wight. Even now it's not what you'd call multicultural, so it was exciting to see such diversity, if not the greatest idea walking all that way when I could have taken the tube. Or more likely, got horribly lost on the tube, the maze that is the London Underground map still a complete mystery at that point.

I walked briskly to the van, quick enough to show that I was keen, but not so fast that the occupants would get any pleasure from me raising a sweat if they took off, perhaps under the impression that they were the first such wits to pull that stunt today. It happens a lot more often than you'd think, but thankfully is rarer than some fuckwit swerving at you for shits and giggles, which also happens with depressing frequency.

The dirt-caked van shudders and shakes, petrol dripping from the exhaust, like it has a runny nose. As I draw closer, the nearside window winds down in jerky movements, its winder obviously as shagged as the rest of the vehicle. Both driver and passenger look harmless enough – student-looking types, roughly my age – the driver wearing a Cure T-shirt and looking, despite his best efforts, almost entirely unlike Robert Smith.

"Leicester?" I ask hopefully.

"Jump in," says Not Robert Smith, motioning to the back of the van.

The rear doors are almost rusted through and behind them is a haze of smoke that I think at first might be hash, but which turns out to be a combination of petrol fumes and patchouli oil. There are also four more student types in the back, which, given that it's a very small van, doesn't leave a lot of room for another passenger, but they ungrudgingly shuffle up and I clamber in as introductions are made, their names forgotten in an instant. Two boys, two girls, one of them with a vague body odour problem.

I sit on the wheel arch on top of my sleeping bag, which is wrapped in a black, plastic bin bag, and we make little conversation, stopping just once to refuel, but it's not like I really want to talk to anyone, content to be thinking of nothing, and more so to be actually moving. The radio drifts between stations, barely audible above the rattle of the van. Progress is slow, but at least it's progress. If nothing else I'll get to Leicester today.

Not that I particularly want to go to Leicester, but it's vaguely part of the deal I made with my mother; before I can be let loose hitching around the country for two weeks, I must first attend the birthday party of a cousin with whom I no longer have anything in common. Ever the black sheep of the family, I am still beholden to their rules so long as I still live with them. I work at a shitty factory job and have two weeks off to do with mostly as I please, but still there are stipulations. Well, one stipulation. Aside from which, they don't seem to care what I get up to, no doubt hoping for the best while expecting the worst.

There are – or were – two cousins, Steven and Paul, and I can't recall which one was having a party. Probably Steven, but it makes no odds now. I learned a few years ago that Paul had died, and it would be rude to speak ill of the dead, not to mention unnecessary since there was no ill will between us. At a young age we'd play together, but those years were long gone even then. It wasn't that I disliked them, we had simply grown apart, their worlds revolving around football and mine around music. Visiting them seemed like a chore.

A couple of hours later Not Robert Smith called back to ask if I wanted the Leicester South junction or the city centre, but I didn't really know. The centre seemed less likely to be wrong, simply because it's in the middle, but it was no better than a guess, my knowledge of Leicester amounting to little more than childhood visits to my grandparents' place. Which was in a different house and more than likely a different part of town. So, city centre it is.

Half an hour later the van rattles and farts off into the warm night air, leaving me outside a piss-filled phone box. I step inside, trying not to breathe the stink in while I dial the number for my aunt and uncle's place, pleasantly surprised that the phone hasn't been vandalised beyond being used as a toilet. A less pleasant surprise is when there's no answer.

Assuming that I'd dialled the wrong number, I try again. It's my cousin's birthday, after all, and they're expecting me, albeit several hours ago. It's not like they would have gone somewhere else. Would they? I let it ring longer this time, allowing for the fact that the party must be underway and maybe they didn't hear the phone. It's still ringing when two blokes stop outside the phone box to light cigarettes, one of them swaying a little as he shields the flame from a non-existent breeze. Aware that my sleeping bag is a bright neon sign that I'm a non-resident of this fair city, and that such a thing is a kicking offence for a lone punk rocker, I do my best to pretend not to have seen them. You'd be surprised how often that works as a form of self-defence.

The phone keeps ringing and still there is no answer. I try to compose my thoughts, but panic begins to set in. Fuck. What am I going to do? I have no idea where they live, nothing but a phone number, and the two blokes are still lurking outside the phone box, so pissed they can barely light their cigarettes. It's Saturday night, pub closing time or thereabouts, not a good time to be out on the street. Closing time means drunks, and drunks don't like punks.

With no other choice I decide to wait, give it five minutes, and try the number again. My mum and step dad are away for the weekend, so I can't call them and check the number, but that wouldn't be an option anyway, admitting failure on my first night. I'd rather sleep in the phone box. Just as I'm thinking that, the two drunk blokes stumble on their way, only to be replaced by two more, both blundering up the street clutching suspicious-looking food stuffs wrapped in greasy paper. The smaller of the two – though they're both bigger than me – presses his face up against the window of the phone box and stares at me.

"Awright, Sid," he burps, glaring through the dirty glass.

The bigger one tugs his sleeve, trying to get him to move on, but he's having none of it.

"'ss Sid Vicious," he growls, apparently annoyed that his friend hasn't recognised me as a deceased Sex Pistol, or perhaps perturbed that he's seen a ghost.

Granted, at the tender age of seventeen I still fashioned myself after Sidney – black leather jacket, spiky hair, and the obligatory padlock and chain – but given that he rather publicly popped his clogs a couple of years ago, it seems like a fairly obvious mistake. This doesn't seem to have occurred to my new friend, however, and he beckons me out of the phone box so he can have a closer look. I don't have a lot of say in the matter. He even holds the door open for me, performing a little jig that he seems to think I'll recognise, but in the process drops a large part of his kebab onto the pavement. There is a brief look of disbelief on his face, and then confusion as he tries to work out why his food is on the ground and whose fault it is. Evidentially he reaches the conclusion that it's my fault.

His friend tugs his sleeve again in an effort to get him moving, home or wherever they were headed, but Kebab Man shrugs him off, studying my face intently. I look him back in the eyes, trying to appear confident, neither scared nor threatening, but he's a nasty-looking bastard, wiry, with shark-cold eyes, and a heavy scar through his left eyebrow. His cheekbones have that puffy, hardened look of someone who's been in frequent punch-ups, and his nose has been broken at least once in the past. He keeps staring and, foolishly, I break eye contact, gazing past his clumpy knuckles at the ground, all the time growing ever expectant of that first sudden movement. I've seen enough random violence against punks to know that it's a distinct possibility. The familiar knot tightens in my stomach, fight or flight, flight being the only realistic option. This fucker looks like he'd win either way, especially since he has me cornered. He slobbers something about punk, incomprehensible, but nonetheless confrontational.

"Leave it, Tone," his friend implores, trying to steer him away with an arm around his shoulder.

They've obviously been through this scene a hundred times before: Tone has hospitalised some poor cunt every weekend since he reached puberty, while his dimwit pal has stood by, too scared, too desperate for friendship, or maybe just too fucking stupid to do anything about it. And tonight it's my turn.

CHAPTER TWO

TONE GLARES AT me, openly hostile.

"That punk rock's a load of shit!" he spits, breathing chilli sauce and onions at me. "Eh, Sid? Fucking shit."

"Yeah, pretty much," I agree resignedly. It's not like he's open to discussion or I could persuade him to check out the new Exploited album, so I may as well agree with him if it stops him from kicking the shit out of me.

"So why," he ponders, attempting to put two and two together and come up with a satisfactory number that means he can hit me, "are you dressed like a cunt?"

Somehow I blurt out a lie. And it's not just a little exaggeration of the truth but a fucking whopper.

"I just ran away from DC," I tell him, trying to sound suitably delinquent, wiping my nose with the back of my hand for added authenticity. "They're looking for someone normal, not some punk wanker."

Tone looks confused. Not, I suspect, a new experience for him.

"We 'ad an outside work party, diggin' holes and that," I blunder on, past the point of no return. "I just walked off when they weren't lookin'."

There is a glimmer of hope: Tone is thinking, a process he is clearly unfamiliar with. You can almost hear the hamster running around on its wheel. Cogs slowly turning. Ice ages passing.

"Portland," I embellish further, immediately regretting it because I know I'm pushing my luck and won't have the correct answers if I'm questioned.

From what little I know of it, Portland Detention Centre is the young offenders equivalent of Alcatraz, an institution where misguided tearaways and yobs become dangerous, fully-fledged criminals. It seems to be where they send all the trouble kids from our village sooner or later, only for them to re-emerge several months later as proper nasty bastards. My friend, Youngy, a fairly harmless layabout, did six months there for a dismal burglary that clearly indicated he was not cut out for a life of crime. Having asked directions to the house he intended to rob, he broke in and stole the stereo before taking it home on the bus, leaving behind him a trail that Stevie Wonder could have followed without too much effort. Clearly he was an arsehole, but he returned from Portland a card-carrying psychopath with delusions of being Ray Winstone. Within days he was inciting bar brawls and trying to stab people in the face, and was quickly on remand for beating the local plod around the head with a length of wood. So much for rehabilitation. Time in Portland is worn as a badge of honour.

"What you in for?" demands Tone, still oozing aggression but the edge in his voice having faded a mere fraction. By his own perverse nutter logic, having escaped from custody, I might be a decent chap after all.

"TDA," I tell him confidently. "I was on probation anyway, so the judge said he wanted to make an example an' that."

Tone's face lights up, visibly less threatening, a knowing smile. The knowledge that I have escaped a custodial sentence for the theft of a car – taking and driving away – and some unspecified previous offence seems, as hoped, to have warmed the cockles of his rather unpleasant heart. It was a calculated risk, but not the first time I've dealt with nutters. Tone is now my friend. He introduces me to the larger oaf, Tweedle Dumber, whose name is also Tony, and having only moments ago been intent of kicking the shit out of me, he is now suddenly concerned about my welfare. Overly concerned, fussing over me like a drunken relative. He gives me a cigarette and a light, and then decides that I should have the whole pack.

"You 'ave 'em, son," he presses the pack into my hand. "You alright for money?" He digs into his pocket and hands over about two quid in loose change.

The problem now is that he won't go away. I try to steer the conversation around to saying goodnight, wishing them well and never seeing them again, but Tone isn't taking the hint. Worse still, his dimwitted sidekick has decided to help by offering a place to lay low for a couple of days, where a friend of his – no doubt also named Tony or some variation thereof – can sort out some fake ID, maybe even a passport. Only moments ago the offer was a new and unrecognisable face, but now the offer seems to include a driving licence and a set of disguises.

Things get even more ridiculous when a police squad car happens past on routine patrol, paying us scant attention. The two Tones make such a big deal out of trying to hide me – standing in front of me and puffing themselves out – that it comes around the block again at a slow cruise, this time eyeing us suspiciously. There's every chance that the cops are actually checking to see if I'm okay and not getting robbed, but I can hardly wave them down to find out. Instead, my best option is to shake these idiots loose, try the phone again and hope to God that someone answers.

Having explained that I'm on my way to a safe house and that help is just a phone call away, I step back inside the phone box and dial the number again. The thicky twins loiter outside, failing once more to take the hint and bugger off. The phone rings. And rings. And rings. Surely the party isn't so loud that they haven't heard the damn thing. And I know it's Leicester and all, but they've had telephones for a while now, so they can't be standing around looking at the strange ringing thing, wondering what the hell to do with it.

Panic sets in again. Only two weeks ago there were riots in the Highfields area of Leicester, and while these particular streets are quiet it wouldn't be wise to be wandering aimlessly with no place to stay, not least because I might unknowingly wander into Highfields. Fuck, I might be in Highfields already, for all I know.

The two Tones are growing restless, no doubt rapidly sobering up. Tony rediscovers his kebab and picks at the greasy remains. Not that he needs the extra fat.

And still the phone rings.

"Hello?"

I'm almost sick with relief. Uncle Peter sounds annoyed at something – probably me – but I explain where I am, giving the address from the label on the phone and even asking directions from the brothers dim, and he says he'll be here in ten minutes.

It doesn't matter now if the goons decide to hang about, I'm quite prepared to spin them more bullshit. In fact, it might be a good idea to keep them here as protection in case any more goons should happen past while I'm waiting. But on hearing that someone's coming to pick me up, they quickly lose interest, and after much shaking of hands, leaving me almost up to the elbow in kebab grease, they finally sod off.

Uncle Peter shows up and throws my stuff in the back seat of his car. He's clearly in a bit of a huff about having to come and get me, not least because he smells of alcohol and probably shouldn't be driving, but it's good to be off the streets, wrapped in a cocoon of family saloon. He explains that the party was being held in a hired hall, which is why no one was in when I called earlier. They'd expected me to arrive this afternoon and when I didn't show up they waited as long as they could. Thankfully it seems I wasn't reported missing, although I'm pretty sure that you have to be gone for 24 hours before anyone takes notice.

He drones on further, his window wound down to allow the breeze to brush against his thick-set face, but I'm not really listening. It's only a short drive, but suddenly I'm so tired that it takes enormous effort to stop from nodding off, like a toddler who's been dashing about all day and then can't stand up. It's been a long day. My stomach gurgles to remind me that it's been fed nothing but a bag of crisps today and would quite like something more substantial. Fat chance since the party's over and all the food will have gone.

Leicester drifts past, drab and uninviting, mostly closed for the night.

And here's an interesting fact: In August 1972 Ugandan president/ despot Idi Amin took it upon himself to expel around 50,000 Asians, giving them just 90 days to get out of the country. In an effort to dissuade the Asians – British passport holders – from moving to their fair city, Leicester City Council launched an advertising campaign in the Uganda Argus, strongly suggesting that they 'not move to Leicester'. Which is a shitty thing to do by any measure, but instead of keeping them away it made more migrants aware of the fact that moving there was even a possibility, and thus had the opposite effect. Which strikes me as most amusing.

But Leicester is not, on the whole, an interesting place. At least not unless you like cricket or football. And I don't. Leicester seems to produce an abundance of players for both these sports and, once upon a time, some notable speedway riders, but nothing much in the way of music, their biggest export besides Queen bassist John Deacon being, rather ironically, an Asian band called Cornershop.

We arrive to find a select few guests that have migrated from the hired hall to the living room for a nightcap, a huddle of balding men in one corner, a gaggle of housewives in the other. Uncle Peter picks up his whiskey glass and his damning of a blind referee where he left it, the inconvenience of my presence already forgotten. Evidently Leicester City Football Club suffered two devastating five-nil defeats at the hands – or rather feet – of Manchester United and Nottingham Forest, but fortunately it's not a conversation in which I'm invited to take part. I have no interest whatsoever in the decisions, right or wrong, of "the wanker in the black" and even less interest in some overpaid cunt chasing a piece of leather around a field. It's not even football season for another couple of weeks.

I'll spare you the details of an uncomfortable few hours at a family gathering, ever the square peg in a round hole, unable and unwilling to join in. Peter, I learned recently, has also passed away, and it's not like he or any of the others did me any wrong. There's no reason to go disturbing any ghosts.

CHAPTER THREE

THE MORNING SUNSHINE, as it lazily seeps through tired net curtains, reveals a panorama of badly made model fighter planes dangling from the ceiling on dusty lengths of cotton thread, their eternal dogfight long forgotten. The room smells of old socks and adolescent sweat, like the locker room for the permed and heavily moustached football players that stare down from every wall, but a room to myself is very much appreciated, my cousins having shared a room for the night. They could just as easily have stuck me on the sofa.

I've spent at least an hour listening for signs of life, but there's been nothing to suggest that anyone's up yet. While it's a safe bet that my auntie Yvonne is the first to rise, I don't want to emerge too early and deal with the uncomfortable feeling of being alone in an unfamiliar house. Or, worse still, have to make conversation about football.

Eventually there are enough noises from downstairs to suggest that the odds are more in my favour, and I amble cautiously downstairs to find everyone up and about, Yvonne making breakfast. She smiles at my arrival, always my favourite auntie, genuinely friendly and concerned about my welfare rather than judgemental of my choices. When she asked last night about my journey to Leicester, why it took so long, I told her the truth about how people would stop their cars and drive away again, hurl abuse, and even swerve at me for a laugh, and she sighed: "I wonder about people sometimes." Which is a lot better than the usual response from others who would suggest that I deserve it for dressing the way I do. "Well, if you'd just dress like a normal person…" Oh, do fuck off!

A couple of hours later I'm back in the same situation, Uncle Peter having dropped me off at the motorway junction. Occasionally a car will stop long enough to wind me up before driving away, while other drivers will take the time to slow down and let me know that I'm a "punk wanker". It gets depressing after a while, but it's not exactly new. Sometimes people are just cunts.

Not that this is the greatest place to get a lift. Another hitchhikers' graveyard. A couple of other hitchhikers – clearly more respectable looking than me – have managed to get rides while I've been waiting, but more still have given up and headed back into town. It would be no surprise to see vultures circling overhead, or perhaps coming down to peck at the corpse of some long dead hippie who waited to death.

Another of Oscar Wilde's offspring yells at me to get a haircut, plainly failing to notice that I already have one, otherwise it wouldn't be standing on end like it is. An hour or so later, a uniformed squaddie shows up and barely has time to stick his thumb out before getting picked up.

"You should smarten yourself up," he grins smugly as he climbs into the passenger seat. "Get yourself a uniform and a haircut."

Again with the fucking haircuts!

And so I wait. And wait. And wait some more. Thumb fishing. No one taking the bait. It's a while longer before I decide to give up and head back into town to the train station, loitering for a few moments in the sure knowledge that, now that I've given up, someone will immediately stop to give me a ride all the way to London, perhaps even drop me off outside the Lyceum. Instead, it starts to spit with rain.

After walking for an hour and a half, I'm pretty much back where I started in Leicester city centre, morning having long given way to afternoon. Another half an hour is wasted finding the station, the same again waiting for a train, but at long last it pulls slowly, haltingly away from this shit stain of a city. Typically, it's one of those trains that seems to stop every ten minutes for no apparent reason, crawling through closed stations when it is actually moving, but eventually it creaks into London St

Pancras and I hurry off towards the tube station, deftly dodging a herd of old ladies who seem to think you win prizes for getting in everyone's way.

The trouble, as I've mentioned, with the London Underground is that the map is largely unintelligible to anyone who doesn't live in London, a spaghetti of different coloured lines with seemingly endless destinations. Once you've got the hang of it, of course, it's fantastic, but until then it's completely baffling, not least because you have to know which station corresponds with your destination. Pre-internet it could be a nightmare, and given that it opened in 1863, with steam powered trains and gas-lit stations, we can only imagine how people found their way around before anyone thought to provide a map.

Actually, that was a bloke called Harry Beck, an engineering drafts-man who designed it in his spare time in 1931, which means almost 70 years without any means of finding your way around. But still you have to know which is the nearest station to where you want to go. Tottenham Court Road? Easy, just go to Tottenham Court Road station. But what if you want to go to Pentonville Road? Is it King's Cross or Angel station? And how the fuck would you be expected to know that in the first place? Get it wrong and you're facing a long walk. And that's one of the simpler routes. Many were the times I stared at that map with not the faintest idea of where I should be going.

Luckily, I know that the Lyceum Ballroom is walking distance from Waterloo station, so I don't have to dither about looking lost and acting like a thief magnet. But even then it's confusing, taking the Northern Line – the black one – north up to Camden Town, before crossing the platform and going south on the same line, because it splits in two and goes in different directions. Surely it's not just me who finds this confusing?

The walk across Waterloo Bridge is sublimely electrifying, the filthy water of the Thames twinkling beneath, as the cityscape stretches off into the distance, the Kinks classic *Waterloo Sunset* inevitably coming to mind. It's not the most attractive bridge, that honour always taken by the majestic Tower Bridge, but no other affords better views or takes you closer to the heart of the city. With the passing of years it would become less special to me, a thoroughfare used only when it was the quickest route, but its shine was never entirely dulled, and crossing it twice in so many days back then – having stopped off to get a gig ticket the day before – was simply thrilling, especially with said gig waiting on the other side.

Perhaps it was the grandeur of the Lyceum as much as the bands that made the gigs there so special. Apparently its origins date back to 1765 and it was the first place to exhibit Madame Tussaud's waxworks, along with hosting the premiere of Mozart's opera *Cosi fan tutte*. Given that the building burned down in 1830, it's not really the same place, just the same site, but the rebuilt venue has an equally rich history, staging everything from Shakespeare to Miss World. Not that I'd have known that at the time, or cared, but it was a great place to see bands and a terrible loss when it closed in the mid-'80s. Indeed, I often wondered what became of the place, having stood empty for so many years, and thanks to the internet I discovered that it was refurbished in 1996 and has been home to the musical version of The Lion King since 1999. The fucking Lion King, night after night! It's not exactly up there with the Clash and the Damned, but perhaps it's understandable that they'd want a rather less boisterous clientèle than a couple of thousand punk rockers gobbing all over the place and throwing beer around.

Tonight, there are punks spilling out of the Wellington pub on the corner of Wellington Street and the Strand, spiky-haired oiks cluttering the pavement, harassing the few passing tourists who haven't crossed the road to avoid them. At the huge wooden doors of the Lyceum stand the huge wooden bouncers, frisking everyone and taking the laces from their boots. It's a pointless exercise; they take your bootlaces so you can't kick anyone, especially them, since the last thing they want is a fair fight. But anyone who's been here before knows what to expect so they bring a spare pair, completely defeating the purpose. And the bouncers must know what's happening, so why bother? Fuck, I don't know, maybe they just collect laces. I imagine bouncers have some pretty strange fetishes.

Having replaced my laces and dumped my sleeping bag off at the cloakroom, I head to the bar for a spot of 'minesweeping', the not-so-noble art of liberating unguarded or abandoned drinks, always sniffing first at the liquid and checking its temperature in case cool lager turns out to be warm piss. There's a reggae band called Talisman on stage, but despite the best efforts of the Clash I have yet to develop such tastes, and would be hard-pushed to name any reggae band beyond Bob Marley and the Wailers. Not that I don't mind the music, eventually even owning a few albums, I'd just rather be listening to punk rock.

By the time the band have finished their set I've 'found' a couple of pints of lager, three quarters of a pint of cider, and a small glass of what tasted rather unpleasantly like gin. I head up to the balcony for further minesweeping, but there are a couple of bouncers up there, off to an early start by battering the shit out of a punk with a green Mohican – or Mohawk as they're now known. One of the bouncers drags him backwards out of his seat, while the other lands shovel-fisted blows that can be heard above the music. He's haemorrhaging blood from his nose as they haul him towards the exit, both still punching him in the face and the back of the head.

A punk girl, presumably his girlfriend returning from the toilet, bravely launches herself at the bigger of the two bouncers, hammering useless punches at him, but he shakes her off like she was a puppy at his ankles. She dives straight back at him, but this merely makes him angry and he grabs her by the throat, disdainfully throwing her to the floor and kicking her in the stomach. She's someone's sister, daughter, girlfriend, maybe mother one day, but he doesn't give a fuck. Big brave man, twice her age and size. The bouncers at the Lyceum are notoriously violent, and one in particular is a horrible cunt, an ugly man in every sense of the word. He served time at least once for assault, only to come out and work the same job. I wish I could remember his name to shame him now, but he'd probably be proud. With any luck he's long dead and hopefully died from something painful.

The girl lies slouched against a table, a rag doll all twisted the wrong way on the filthy, beer stained carpet, her make-up all smudged like a bad Alice Cooper. Her boyfriend tries to curl up into a ball as he's manhandled out of sight, but he's still gasping for breath from a punch or kick that knocked the wind out of him. No one lifts a finger to help. It's not that no one cares, it's just that no one knows him, he's not with any mates who'll watch his back or risk a similar kicking trying to save him. He's just in the wrong place at the wrong time. A girl in torn fishnets and an Exploited

T-shirt goes to help the dazed girlfriend. She probably needs an ambulance, but the chances are slim that anyone will call one.

Pretty much every week some unsuspecting punter is beaten senseless for a heinous crime like sitting in the wrong seat or returning a bouncer's glance, and nine times out of ten the bouncers get away with it because they pick on the right people. Some lone kid who's travelled fifty miles or more to see his favourite band. Someone who nobody's going to stand up for. Grown men with leaded gloves beating up teenagers. My turn had yet to come, but as you can imagine it is not something I will ever forget.

Afraid that I'll be next if I linger too long alone, I head back downstairs to the relative sanctuary of the back bar, where the bouncers rarely cause problems with customers who are buying drinks and who, more to the point, might be able to give them a fair fight or press charges against them.

There are a dozen or so psychobillies standing in a pack, admiring each other's tattoos, but they're not a threat so long as you don't rile them, and standing nearby means I enjoy the safety of their numbers. Even the bouncers aren't stupid enough to pick on large gangs, always selecting easy prey among the lone punks from out of town, some primitive instinct leading them to the weakest of the herd. Pshychobillies, being at least tolerant of punks – some of them ex-punks themselves – offer some protection for now, both from bouncers and the few skinheads here tonight, but it only lasts until the Meteors come on and they all head for the front to knock the shit out of each other. A couple of them leave half pints behind, so I wait a few moments in case they come back, and then claim them as my own.

Intent on getting as close to the heart of the music as possible, I head to the front of the stage as soon as the Meteors finish their set. There's already a row of punks pressed up against the barrier and no amount of unobtrusive wriggling is going to fit another one in, but the second row is good enough. Besides, I can live without another line of bruises across my ribs from being pressed up against the barrier by the weight of the crowd behind me. Already that weight is building, the crowd packed tighter and tighter, until it's impossible to move, and there is a moment of guilty pleasure in being wedged in behind a pretty punk girl, our contact so close as to be unavoidably sexual. I can smell her perfume, feel the heat from her body, as the sway of the crowd pushes us together, tension and anticipation building as we wait for the band.

I won't pretend to remember Killing Joke's setlist, but with just two albums at that time, the self-titled debut and the recently released *What's This For?*, it would probably have leaned heavily on the former, with a handful of songs from the new record and even the early singles. Either way, Killing Joke have rarely been anything less than spectacularly intense, Geordie disdainfully pumping out riffs that have been endlessly plagiarised ever since, while Jaz Coleman does his wild-eyed madman thing, beneath a layer of warpaint, a truly exceptional frontman for a truly exceptional band. Not to mention a sharp poke in the eye to those dunderheads who claim that punk was a spent force by '79 or ended when the Clash signed to CBS. For some reason, that makes me unutterably angry. I know it shouldn't, but it does. I shall refrain from ranting about it.

When the house lights finally come back on at the end, I shuffle across the sea of broken plastic glasses that carpets the dance floor, my ears ringing from the show as I keep an eye out for lost treasure; studs, badges, jewellery... I swear no one actually buys this stuff, they just recycle it at gigs. Not that there's much worth salvaging tonight beyond a few safety pins and a white pill of unknown origins, which I pocket just in case it turns out to be saleable.

Outside, having retrieved my sleeping bag from the cloakroom, I scan the crowded street for familiar faces. Usually I'd head across the bridge to get the late train and the early ferry home, but tonight I am alone with nowhere to go. It's time to spend my first night sleeping rough in London.

CHAPTER FOUR

A STEADY STREAM of punks pours out from between the vast, white pillars at the entrance of the Lyceum, but no one I recognise apart from the known nutters who it's best to avoid eye contact with, a timely reminder that I need to find somewhere safe to sleep tonight. I could do without getting robbed by feral skinheads on my first night in the wild. Not that there were any more than a handful at the show, Killing Joke attracting a more cerebral audience, but that doesn't mean the streets are safe from other varieties of thugs.

I'm still hanging around trying to figure out where I should go when a slap on my shoulder nearly makes me jump out of my skin. A familiar cackle stops me from making a fool of myself and taking off like a greyhound. Danny Brain Damage is standing behind me, giggling like a naughty child, with about half a dozen of the Winchester punks loitering nearby. Quite how I missed them is anyone's guess, but they're a welcome sight nonetheless, exactly the kind of faces I was looking for.

"Fucking hell, you made me jump!" I tell Danny, redundantly.

"Sorry," he says, clearly not in the least.

I first met Danny and the Winchester crew about a year previous, while we were all waiting for that late train out of Waterloo, none of us with any money or tickets, since there is never a ticket inspector to be seen at three o'clock in the morning. There's an air of mischief about them that upsets the general public no end, but never seems to get out of hand or lead to serious trouble. They get out of nasty situations with meathead thugs by talking friendly gibberish at them until they just sort of go off the idea of violence and wander off looking confused. And while they're often badly behaved and stand out like, well, like a gang of snot-nosed punk rockers acting like baboons in an empty train station, they always manage to keep it together when the cops arrive. The glue bags disappear and the bawdy language becomes polite, if slightly cheeky banter. Few cops can resist the charm of these harmless oiks, which no doubt reminds them of the Bash Street Kids, and every time I've been with them in these situations we get a gentle ticking off and the cops leave us in peace.

They're a tight-knit bunch, all instantly likeable, with Danny as the obvious clown and ringmaster, built like a broom handle, with dirty, blond hair that looks like it was cut as a practical joke while he was asleep, random clumps missing and sticking out in all directions. That he still has the same haircut suggests that he did it on purpose. He's also a walking pharmacy, always with a stash of assorted drugs hidden in the recesses of the grubby and unpleasantly stained flasher's mac that he wears all the time. If he doesn't kill himself experimenting with some bizarre substance previously only tested on laboratory rats, he'll probably go on to become a brilliant artist or something. Or perhaps a comedian, a foul-mouthed Norman Wisdom. That first night, and many nights after, when we weren't swapping jokes or talking about bands, he kept us entertained, and passers-by horrified, with his weird contortionist act, walking around the station on his hands, with his legs wrapped around the back of his head, like some ridiculous mutant crab.

He produces a glue bag from nowhere, like a cheap magician pulling a long-dead rabbit from a hat, and offers me a go on it while he examines the pill I found this evening.

"Don't recognise this one," he ponders while I inhale Evostick fumes, getting an instant buzz. "Looks like it might be a downer, like Secanol or something, but I'm not really sure. You got any more?"

"No, just that one," I tell him, passing the glue bag back. "I found it. Just wondered if it was worth taking."

"Well, there's only one, so it won't kill you," he reasons, turning it over as if searching for further clues.

"Don't suppose you want to swap it for anything?"

"Not really, mate," he shrugs. "I s'pose I could try it for research purposes…"

"Swap it for a bag of glue?"

"You drive a hard bargain, sir," Danny grins like a dodgy car sales-man, never one to turn down a deal. "But because it's you, I'll make it a fresh bag."

We exchange drugs, Danny like a card sharp with a marked deck, slip-ping my pill into one pocket and smoothly producing a tin of Evostick from another, like he's playing a rather dubious game of 'find the lady'.

"I take it sir doesn't have his own bag?"

"No, sir doesn't, but I'm sure you have a spare one."

"Indeed," he grins, dipping into yet another pocket and pouring a generous helping of the sticky stuff for me. "And will sir be joining us in the station tonight?"

It's a simple question, to which the answer would normally be yes, but tonight it merely serves to highlight the fact that I'll be alone in the big, bad city, easy prey for the aforementioned nutters if I don't find a safe place to spend the night.

For the Winchester crew, and usually for me, too, that bright-lit station is a place to wind down after a gig, ears still ringing and sweaty T-shirts slowly drying, safe among friends until that last train takes us home. And although I've always felt a little excluded, the only one of our number to stay on until the end of the line, still dealing with ferries and the long, long walk alone, hours after they're all tucked up in bed, I have always felt welcomed by them. Part of something, if only for a couple of hours. Tonight there's no train to take me anywhere and for a moment, if not for the first time today, I feel lost and vulnerable and slightly afraid. It would be fun to hang around with them for a few hours, but when their train left I'd be stuck at the station, a sitting duck for late night psychos, drunks, and bored cops. Experience has taught me to be out of sight in the long, dark hours, hiding from vampires until sunrise.

"Nah, not tonight, mate," I tell Danny, trying to sound more confident than I feel. Brave little soldier. Stupid little cunt. "I'm staying in London."

Thankfully, Danny doesn't know or care enough to push the issue, otherwise I'd be easily persuaded to join them for a few hours. But with the crowds beginning to thin around us, the rest of the crew are growing restless, perhaps knowing that the station is a safer place to be hanging around, if only because it's brightly lit and a few steps closer to home. So I say my goodbyes, glancing wistfully after them as they amble towards the bridge, Danny leading them like some drug-addled Pied Piper, aping the John Wayne walk of an over-sized psychobilly in front of them. The stream of faces leaving the venue has slowed to a trickle and I almost reconsider going to the station, but think better of it, and instead stride purposefully, always purposefully, off towards the Strand, with absolutely no idea where I'm going.

I huff greedily on the glue bag for a few moments, just enough to start getting a good buzz, and then think better of that, too. Now is probably not the best time to be stumbling about, hallucinating wildly and dribbling all over myself. Glue is an incapacitating drug that can take the mind wherever it chooses while you hang on for the ride, and like all hallucinogens it's best done in a relatively safe environment, or at least among friends. This is definitely not the time or place to be growing extra arms that flail about uselessly or, worse still, extra legs that won't obey you when you tell them to run from a gang of thick-skulled boneheads. Glue offers far more vivid hallucinations than magic mushrooms, or even acid. Moreover, it's a drug that's used to kill boredom – not to mention brain cells – and the last thing I am right now is bored.

Just up ahead I spot some stragglers from the gig, two girls and a boy, all three carrying sleeping bags. I quicken my pace a little to catch up, but not enough that it looks deliberate; it's not like they're going anywhere in a hurry. They break step when I draw closer, naturally wary, but the girls – both fat and bulging out of fishnets and miniskirts – offer warm, giggly smiles. The boy, however, a nerdy-looking student type, with greasy hair that flops over his eyes, looks like he's going to run away. I'm not sure what from or where to, but he's clearly very scared. I smile at him, reassuring. No threat here. He backs away, a frightened little rabbit. For fuck's sake! How has this cunt survived a Killing Joke gig?

Even though he's roughly the same age as me I feel a bit sorry for him, cowering and cringing at every passing stranger. It's probably his first time in London – up from the suburbs, away from his parents, out in the bright lights – and it can be overwhelming if you've never been here before, a stark contrast even to small cities let alone towns and villages. Unfortunately he has yet to learn the most basic lesson for survival here, which is never to show fear.

Admittedly, it's much easier said than done, but like moths to a midnight flame, this poor sod, frightened of his own shadow, will attract exactly the kind of nutters he's so afraid of. Nutters can smell fear like dogs, and the more he tries not to be here the more he stands out and the more trouble he'll attract. And then, next time he comes back – if he ever comes back – he'll be even more afraid and attract even more trouble. The cruellest irony being that he's entirely nondescript and doesn't stand out at all. If he wasn't making such a fuss, no one would even notice him.

If not for wetting my toes with gigs in Portsmouth and Southampton, I guess I could have gone the same way the first time I came to London, but I was far too excited to be frightened of anything much. Besides which, I've learned through experience that some backwater town can be just as scary as any city, far too many cunts trying to be big fish in a small pond. It's funny how many supposed hard cases have moved to London, then come running back home with their tail between their legs a few weeks later, because they were hopelessly out of their depth. But instead of teaching them any sort of humility it just makes them more pointlessly territorial, more bitter, more threatening. Dangerous failures.

I smile again, trying to put him at ease, but the hit of glue, on top of several pints, has rendered me temporarily incapable of saying anything useful. Calm down, you stupid cunt. I'm not the enemy. I'm not the beating that you're so utterly petrified of. I know that fear, but I am not the cause of it. How can you not see that?

It's then that I realise I'm still holding a glue bag, probably reeking of the stuff, which is not the best party invite in polite – or even impolite – circles. Along with Tuinal, our dear friend Evostick is generally the drug of choice for mental cases who have no use whatsoever for the brain cells they're killing in their thousands with each fresh hit. Seriously, it's a massacre in there! Genocide! You can actually feel the fuckers dying! But mind expansion is not the point; the point is a cheap horror show of wild hallucinations, nothing more. No wonder student boy is scared, he thinks I'm one of the nutters!

Which suggests that he has also failed to learn the other important lesson for survival, that of identifying said nutters and telling them apart. Is it the common or garden football nutter who might be persuaded not to kick your face in if you support the right team? Or perhaps the ageing Teddy Boy who is easily outrun because he's out of shape and smokes too much? The former will probably catch you if you leg it, since he might get more exercise. The latter can be laughed at from a safe distance, providing you can be certain of never seeing him again. Your skinhead, meanwhile, *calvitium vulgaris*, is rarely hostile unless found in a large pack, otherwise known as a thicket.

Thankfully, the two girls don't seem remotely bothered and, still giggling, they introduce themselves as Catherine and Denise. Their friend, though neither explains whether he's a friend, little brother, or just some twat they've got stuck with, is called Graham. We walk along the Strand in a row of three, me on the outside nearest the road, the girls on the inside, and Graham a few paces behind, bravely taking care that his shadow doesn't jump him.

"Where are you headed?" I ask, now the head rush has passed.

"Dunno," shrugs Catherine, the larger of the two girls, but only if comparing an elephant to a hippopotamus. "We might doss in the park."

"Mind if I tag along?"

"S'pose so," Catherine shrugs again, an ungainly lolloping movement, like someone throwing a blancmange at a plate.

"You'll have to shag her though," Denise chips in. "It's her birthday."

They giggle again, perhaps at some inside joke, and I laugh along with them, mostly at the idea that anyone would attempt to fuck either of them without the aid of half a dozen Sherpas and a mountain rescue team. They really are very large.

Admittedly, Denise would be quite pretty if she wasn't only slightly smaller than a London bus, but Catherine, alas, has all the sex appeal of something that's washed up on a beach, one of those unidentified sea creatures that baffles scientists. Is it a whale? No, it has a beak. Perhaps a giant squid? No, it has arms and legs.

Of course, one should never judge people by their looks. It's what's on the inside that counts. Unless you're expected to put your dick inside them. Although, on reflection, perhaps this explains why the kid behind us is such a bundle of nerves. Maybe he knows something I don't.

CHAPTER FIVE

WE CROSS THE lower end of Trafalgar Square, surprisingly empty even of drunks, and amble through the imposing Admiralty Arch, turning left on The Mall into St James's Park. It would be nice to suggest that I knew, then, that the arch was built in 1912, commissioned by King Edward VII in memory of his mother, Queen Victoria. But, of course, I didn't have the faintest idea and probably, almost certainly, wouldn't have cared. Indeed, it's a surprise to find out that it's a relatively new construction, and somewhat appalling to learn that it's since been given over to hotel development and fancy apartments. At the time I didn't even know there was a park on the other side of the arch, fifty-seven acres of it, less still that London has so many parks that it technically qualifies as a forest.

St James's Park, itself, has an interesting history, of which I knew nothing then, dating back to 1532 when Henry VIII bought an area of marshland, which was then drained and landscaped under the reign of James I. Not, I hasten to add, the James for whom the park was named: that, apparently, was James The Less, some Biblical fella. Or rather, the park was named for a leper hospital, which was named for James The Less. And, yes, of course I had to look this stuff up.

By all accounts, the park was home to all manner of exotic animals, including camels, crocodiles, and even an elephant. But more interesting still, and rather more germane, is the fact that the park became notorious for 'acts of lechery' as evidenced by a poem entitled A Ramble In St James's Park by John Wilmot, which begins with the immortal line, 'Much wine

had passed, with grave discourse. Of who fucks who, and who does worse.'
The poem then goes on to describe rape, buggery, and incest, employing
the word 'cunt' no less than eight times. Given that he died at thirty-three
from syphilis and alcoholism, Wilmot knew what he was talking about.

We unroll our sleeping bags under a cluster of trees by the lake and
sit making small talk in hushed voices, while the capital's traffic rumbles
like distant thunder. It's almost disconcerting being in the heart of the city
and yet unable to hear much more than the occasional passing truck, and
no wonder we find ourselves talking so quietly. Although not as quiet as
Graham, who still hasn't spoken a word.

Cigarettes are smoked below the butt and we lay back in our sleeping bags, gazing at the night sky through the trees. With the city's light
pollution no stars are visible, but it's warm enough that we barely need
the sleeping bags, not even a breeze to disturb the leaves above. Which is
curious, because nearby there's a gentle rustling sound like a plastic bag
blowing in the wind.

I glance to my right to see Denise in her sleeping bag, wriggling across
the grass towards me like some giant science fiction pupa, a badly made
Doctor Who alien. She reaches my side, in one swift move unzips my
own sleeping bag to the waist and, without so much as a please or thank
you, plunges her hand down the front of my jeans. I barely have time to
protest – or at least consider whether I'm going to protest or not – before
she's expertly jettisoned her clothes and climbed on top of me, all but
pinning me to the ground. With no encouragement whatsoever she then
starts writhing up and down, making strange guttural noises, which I fear
can be heard all over London.

Or maybe not, because somewhere in the near distance is another
noise, faint at first, muted by the trees, but growing rapidly louder. A
song perhaps? Drunks singing in Trafalgar Square? Denise continues her
unprovoked groaning and the song returns. No, not a song, a chant. It
grows louder still, coming this way. Oh shit!

"Skinheads! Skinheads! Skinheads!"

They appear from between the trees not more than fifty feet away,
about a dozen of them stomping towards the lake, silhouettes of shaved
heads and steel toe-capped boots. I hiss at Denise to shut the fuck up,

clamping my hand over her mouth, but she seems to have got the message, quiet as a mouse now, if not, alas, the same size. Over to our right, partially hidden by the sleeping megalith that is Catherine, Graham has curled up into the foetal position, whimpering like a beaten puppy, his fear, for once, entirely justified. The skinheads haven't spotted us yet, but they're clearly in the mood to kick the shit out of something, their play-fighting bordering on unarmed combat.

Or at least it was unarmed until one of them notices a large stack of deck chairs by the lake, which they set about dismantling with surprising zeal, kicking at them in the half-darkness until they are each equipped with bludgeon-sized lengths of wood, with which they can vigorously thwack each other. To celebrate this monumental achievement they break into another round of "Skinheads! Skinheads!", followed by a bout of "Sieg Heil!", and just for good measure – though considerably more worrying – a catchy little ditty entitled 'We Hate Punks'.

Denise lays motionless on top of me, a dead weight, making it difficult to breathe let alone make a run for it. At this rate I'll suffocate long before the skinheads get the chance to kill us, and for a brief moment the headline of tomorrow's *Sun* flashes past my mind: PORKY PUNK IN SEX DEATH SHOCKER! This is not how I want to die, trapped and gasping for air beneath the European sex mountain. Although, all things considered, it beats getting kicked to death by skinheads.

Somehow the skinheads still haven't spotted us, their 'We Hate Punks' routine apparently just a practice run in case they should happen to find any. Like, for instance, less than fifty feet away, cowering in their sleeping bags. Thankfully, Catherine has stopped snoring and Graham has yet to leg it off towards Trafalgar Square, leaving me trapped and Denise with her buttocks exposed to the moon, a glowing beacon for violation. In other circumstances it might actually be funny, but not more than a few months ago a fifteen-year-old punk was killed in Southampton after skinheads chased him onto wasteland, put him under a petrol-soaked mattress, and set him on fire. I read that the body could only be identified by the dog chain he was wearing around his neck and what was left of his leather jacket. It's not the first such horror story and it won't be the last, but I have no intention of becoming a chapter in that book. Then again, neither did he. He was just in the wrong place at the wrong time, as we are tonight.

Still oblivious to our presence, the deckchair army tire of whacking each other with pieces of wood and decide that it would be a good idea to throw the smallest of their number into the lake. There is a surprisingly quiet splash as the unfortunate bonehead disappears beneath the surface, but I take the opportunity to wriggle free of Denise and slip out of my sleeping bag, at least allowing the option to run away if we're spotted. I don't have to outrun the skinheads, just, as the old adage goes, outrun Catherine, Denise and Graham. If the worst comes to the worst, I'll lose my boots, my sleeping bag and my dignity, but retain my teeth.

The bonehead surfaces, hollering abuse at his cohorts, glistening as he clambers from the water. Evidently he is not pleased about the dunking, employing the C-word almost as enthusiastically as Wilmot, but there wasn't really much he could do to prevent it. At least it won't take long for his hair to dry.

Eventually the skinheads grow bored and wander off the way they came, noisily and with their knuckles scraping the ground. Silence descends once more, spoiled only by the ever present ringing in my ears from the gig. I lay still, heart rate returning to normal now that the danger has gone, and that weird sense of elation, the adrenaline rush that comes with having escaped danger. Once again there is peace.

Moments later Catherine clambers to her feet, stomps over to Denise, and kicks her hard in the chest.

"You fucking cow!" she spits, before marching back to her sleeping bag.

Apparently she had been awake the whole time, lying there, bitter and resentful, as Denise moaned and groaned like a badly dubbed porn film. It was supposed to be her that got shagged on her birthday. I'm just thankful we didn't all get fucked.

CHAPTER SIX

CATHERINE ISN'T TALKING to Denise. Denise isn't talking to Catherine. Graham isn't talking to anyone. No one is talking to me. Together we trudge out of the park, back through Admiralty Arch and into the hustle of London's busy streets, the traffic doing its best to disguise our silence. I don't even know why I'm going with them, except that it's easier to follow someone than to make any sort of decision about where I'm going to go today.

Catherine and Denise both hate me because they've fallen out with each other about who did or didn't get laid. And somehow it's all my fault. They glare daggers at me, which, in the cold light of day, are particularly ugly daggers. Granted, I'm probably not looking my best, but these two have all the allure of a couple of cement mixers, and personalities to match. Although, at least they have personalities, which is more than can be said for Graham, skulking along behind us. Moping cunt.

Luckily my reluctant companions' wandering is less aimless than my own and we somehow end up at Victoria Coach Station, roughly a mile and a half from the park, but an entirely different world, busy and bustling, belching diesel fumes. While the others walk off to recheck timetables, our goodbyes less than cordial, I fish a soiled copy of last week's *Sounds* out of a bin and scan the gig guide for something to do tonight, starting first with London where there appears to be nothing of worth, and then moving to alphabetic order. Aberdeen, too far. Bridlington, don't know where it is, Cardiff, Carlisle, Dover… A huge bundle of fuck all. Perhaps not surprising given that today is Monday.

I'm suddenly aware that I have company peering over my shoulder, trying to read the guide with me. I look up and a green-haired oik looks back at me. Black leather jacket, Sid Vicious swastika T-shirt, jeans torn at the knees, scuffed Docs…

"Gis ten pee for a cup of tea," he suggests, cheerfully.

"No."

He shrugs and I look back at the gig guide. Edinburgh. Exeter. Farnham. Frome… Where the fuck is Frome?

"Where y' goin'?" he enquires, scrutinising something he's just picked out of his ear.

I consider for a moment, still with no real idea. Anywhere but here. And then I spot it.

"Southend," I tell the oik. "See Siouxsie and the Banshees."

"Banshees, yeah?" the oik's face lights up. "I know them. I'll come with you, yeah? I can get us in for nuffin. You goin' on the coach?"

What do you think, numb-nuts? Actually, the question's not as foolish as it seems. I have no clue how to get to Southend from here, but since we're in a coach station it might not be the worst idea.

"Yeah."

The oik introduces himself as Neil, shaking my hand in his dirt-sticky palm, and we go to check the timetables. Neil then goes off to ponce his ticket fare, which, in layman's terms, means harassing tourists for money. Possibly he has some pre-concocted, heart-rending tale with which to fleece said tourists of their cash – his dear old mother being on her death bed or some such bullshit – but more likely he just demands spare change. Either way, he's back within twenty minutes.

He reminds me of the Artful Dodger, a cheeky London scallywag who says "Yeah?" at the end of almost every sentence. All he needs is a top hat and a pocketful of stolen handkerchiefs to complete the ensemble. I don't trust the fucker as far as I can spit him, but half an hour later we're on a coach to Southend, sharing a bottle of wine that tastes like paint stripper. Apparently, he stole it.

The coach journey, just under two hours, is as much fun as such journeys can be, Neil and I jabbering away about nothing important, half pissed by the time we get to Southend. We stumble off the coach and Neil immediately skulks off to steal another bottle from the nearest off-licence. In a breeze that reeks of decaying fish, we sit on the seawall and stare out at the dishwater sea. It's not even midday.

"Least you nicked a decent one this time," I tell Neil, passing the bottle back. "That last stuff was fucking horrible."

"It's the same stuff," he grunts. "Strongest one, innit."

We sit for a while longer, daydreaming. There's hours to kill before the gig and nothing to do but wait. No point even hanging around outside the venue, since there won't be anyone there yet. But it's not like we have any pressing engagements beyond maybe getting a bag of chips, stealing more wine, and going for a wander along the famous – and remarkably flammable – Southend pier.

Indeed, while it might be the longest pleasure pier in the world, at nearly a mile and a half long, Southend pier seems to be cursed with catastrophically bad luck. First, the pavilion at the shore end of the pier was destroyed by fire in 1959, causing 500 people to be rescued by boat. Then another fire, in 1976, destroyed much of the pier head, followed by yet another blaze in 1977, which damaged the bowling alley. Then, a couple of years later, a boat crashed into the new pier head causing major structural damage and leaving a 70-foot gap. And then – I'm not making this up – the bowling alley burned down in 1995. Oh, and there was another fire in 2005.

So we didn't go for a walk along the pier that day, just sat and looked at it for a while and drank shitty wine. But there are worse ways to spend a day. In the real world I'd have been at work since nine. Monday morning, bored out of my fucking skull, watching the clock, waiting, waiting, waiting to go to a home where I don't feel at home. Still with five days to go before the weekend. With three million unemployed, one in ten of the population, I'm frequently told that I'm lucky to have a job at all, but working nine to five for less than I'd get on the dole doesn't strike me as particularly fortunate. Sitting here doing nothing seems like a far better deal.

"I fuckin' 'ate skinheads."

"Huh?"

"Skinheads, yeah?" repeats Neil, breaking the trance. "I fuckin' 'ate 'em."

He nods almost imperceptibly down the promenade, and there, off in the distance, is a swarm – or thicket – of at least fifty skinheads. They're not in any hurry, but they're coming this way.

Today, if you google Southend-on-Sea, 1981, the first half a dozen images that come up are of skinheads, which then leads to dozens more links, invariably with a gang of these fuckwits throwing Nazi salutes or kicking the shit out of somebody. The truly scary thing is they're still out there somewhere, grown men with kids of their own, and in recent years they've started crawling out of the woodwork again, emboldened by the politics of hate. There were thousands of the bastards, every town infested with them, and it's not like they all died of some Nazi plague. Like cock-roaches scuttling under a sideboard, they must have gone somewhere, only to re-emerge years later with the same ugly rhetoric and no idea how to spell it, still too fucking stupid to realise that they'd be first against the wall. Yes, mate, of course that immigrant doctor took your job.

In 1981 they were everywhere, and while a rose-tinted, revisionist history would have you believe that they were generally harmless and non-racist, the truth is rather different. By '81, the original reggae-loving skins of the '60s were long gone, and in their stead were hordes of knuckle-dragging thugs festooned with swastika tattoos. I met perhaps three or four non-racist skins during those years, one of whom would go with me on anti-apartheid marches. But they were few and far between and, for obvious reasons, difficult to tell apart until they were uncomfortably close, even assuming that you're familiar with the intricacies of skinhead bootlace etiquette. There is no small irony in the fact that the most homophobic of them were usually gay, queer bashing because they were too cowardly to be open about their own sexuality. Oh, but these were different times. It wasn't safe to walk around being openly gay. Yeah, because of you, you cunts.

In fairness, they seem to have got their house in order in recent years, but it will be a long time before that ugly stain is gone. Suffice to say, I shared Neil's intense dislike of the bald brethren.

"Shall we go and find the venue?" I suggest casually.

"No point," reminds Neil, offering me one of my own cigarettes that somehow seem to have come from his pocket. "Won't be no one there yet. Prob'ly won't load the gear in 'til about three."

I light my cigarette, put the packet back in my own pocket, and glance nervously at the approaching crop-headed thunder. If we just nonchalantly started ambling off in the opposite direction they'd never even notice us, much less bother to give chase. Leave it too long and not only will we be right on their path but we'll have given up a head start. Neil senses my growing apprehension.

"Don't worry about it," he insists. "They won't do nuffin."

That they won't do nuffin is precisely what I'm worried about.

Neil takes a deep lungful of nicotine, sucking the life out of his cigarette. He doesn't seem at all bothered, totally unconcerned. I glance back down the seafront, no head movement, just eyeballs straining to see how long we've got before they reach us. There isn't much time.

I take a deep swig on the bottle of Dutch courage and painkiller. The skins are getting close enough that one or two of the faster ones would probably catch us if we fled. Neil takes the bottle from me, swigging on it lightly, but I suspect wanting to hold onto it as a potential weapon. He speaks in a low croak, practically inaudible: "Just ignore 'em, yeah? Look straight ahead and ignore 'em. They won't do nuffin."

Another drag on the cigarette.

I can hear boots now, dozens of them. Close. Only yards away. Then the first steps draw level, directly behind us, clumping past. I can feel the eyes boring into the back of our heads. Hatred. Neil casually passes me the bottle and I drain its contents, getting an unwanted view of bald heads as I do so. Every one of them is looking at us as they pass, contempt in their eyes. And yet still there is no violence.

The last in the herd, a stunted little shit who looks like he's about twelve years old, gobs at me as he passes, but a sudden gust of wind takes his offering back and lands it on his sleeve. His step falters for a second as he considers his next move; surely we ought to have the crap kicked out of us for getting spit on his new Harrington jacket, but the others don't seem to have noticed and they keep walking, leaving him a few paces behind. Too young – too short of hair – to do anything on his own, he quickens his pace in case the odds against him change as suddenly as the breeze.

Neil lets out a sigh that turns into an unhealthy cough. He spits the results onto the beach, a horrible brown oyster, and then, with a sly grin, motions over his shoulder at the two cop vans that are following the skinheads at a slow crawl. I can't help laughing, mostly out of relief; all the time, Neil knew we were reasonably safe and that if we'd run for it we'd have looked foolish. Instead, we look relatively cool, just sitting there drinking wine with not a care in the world. And perhaps more to the point, I'm not stuck hanging around with a lunatic who doesn't know when to run away.

"Better watch our backs tonight, yeah?" Neil steals another of my cigarettes, lighting it with my Bic, which somehow seems to have found its way to his pocket. "Bet your life they're goin' to the gig."

An unfortunate turn of phrase.

CHAPTER SEVEN

CLIFFS PAVILION IS an oddly-shaped building that sits, as the name suggests, on the edge of a small cliff, overlooking the mouth of the Thames estuary and the North Sea. With a capacity of around 1,600 it was opened in 1964, and continues to host a huge variety of music, everything from pantomime to punk. Sometimes both on the same night, although that's not necessarily intentional.

Some hours later, I find myself sitting outside the place waiting for Neil to return. He's been gone for quite a while, supposedly sorting us out free tickets, but if he doesn't show up soon then I might have to consider buying a ticket. Or sneaking in if the gig's sold out. It's not like I called the venue to check. Thankfully, he reappears about fifteen minutes later, grinning from ear to ear.

"Sorted, yeah?" he informs as if he's asking. "Le's go an' get some more wine."

We get back to the venue about half an hour after the doors have opened and sure enough there are two free tickets at the box office, along with a couple of VIP passes that allow us access to a private box on the balcony. Clearly Neil wasn't kidding about knowing the right people. Unfortunately, it immediately becomes clear that a large number of the audience is made up of the wrong people, and this could be a really long night. Or a really fucking short one.

John Cooper Clarke is up first, a 'punk poet' from Salford, atonal and nasal, like his nose has been broken. Which it may well be tonight, if he doesn't keep the boneheads amused. It helps that he rhymes 'tank' with 'wank', but the rest is probably a little too highbrow for those of the audience who have just one brow. It's not long before they become bored and restless. Which is not a good sign. Few things are more volatile than a bunch of bored skinheads. Regrettably, their mood is not further enhanced by the showing of a 1978 animation by Geoff Dunbar entitled Ubu, which features huge, blubbery beasts committing acts of gratuitous violence and screeching at each other for about twenty minutes. It also involves reading, which will not sit well with some of the slower-witted skinheads.

"It's gonna kick off in a minute," observes Neil, employing skills in detection that wouldn't put a chimpanzee out of work. Obviously it's going to kick off.

We retreat to the bar, which, if nothing else, is better lit and thus very slightly less likely to be a venue for violence. But we can't hide here all night. Ubu has reached, rather fittingly, Act 7: The Battle. Tension fills the air. In unspoken agreement, Neil and I decide that it's time to go and see what these passes do, and we head upstairs.

And not a moment too soon. We peer down over the side of the private box and almost directly below us a small fistfight is rapidly developing into a large brawl. A ripple of violence becomes a wave as it spreads out across the dance floor, with people moving quickly out of its path and others charging in, the latter being boneheads throwing cowardly kicks and sucker punches. The action stops as it started, suddenly and for no apparent reason, but there can be little doubt that we haven't seen the last of it.

For a while the tension subsides, just the hum of chatter above the background music. It's strange being up here, disconnected, like royal guests – or more accurately, like a punk Statler and Waldorf from the Muppet Show – but as soon as the lights dim and the Banshees appear on stage the mood turns nasty again and a fresh skirmish breaks out on the far side of the hall. It fails to spread this time, a brief scuffle as someone gets punched a few times and beats a hasty retreat. I'm glad we're not down there.

The Banshees, for what it's worth, are incredible, jagged and intense as they offer a set that leans towards the newly released *Juju* album. Listening to it now for the first time in decades it has lost none of its edge and sits easily amongst the finest records of its kind, but it's safe to say that the boneheads are not here for the music. Indeed, as Siouxsie says in the 2003 biography by Mark Paytress, the band grew increasingly pissed off by their presence and tried everything to deter them, "…drawing attention to them and slagging them off, even stopping gigs and beating the shit out of them a few times. But they just wouldn't fuck off."

In hindsight, perhaps the band brought it upon themselves, first with Siouxsie's casual use of the swastika on her clothing, and then by provoking the boneheads with Star of David imagery, but either way it became a constant thorn in their side. Not to mention a nightmare for anyone who actually wanted to see them play. Tonight they're no more than two or three songs into the set before the "Sieg Heil" chants start up, hundreds of arms rising out of the middle of the crowd in a synchronised salute. Another fight breaks out and the band stop playing and appeal for calm. Which is rather like appealing to the tide not to come in.

But someone, it seems, will be getting wet tonight.

Giggling as he drains the last of his pint, Neil unzips his jeans and starts pissing into the empty glass. The band start playing again but directly below us, joined by a single braincell, half a dozen arms are still raised in the Nazi salute. The same gang that started the previous fight. Neil finishes pissing, almost a full pint, and has to put the glass down while he controls his laughing fit. It doesn't take a genius to see what he's planning. He's going to get us killed.

The first skinhead wipes a light splash from the back of his head and scowls at the space behind him as we duck back for cover. The next dribble has two boneheads scrutinising the crowd around them, looking puzzled and angry, which is not, I suspect, a new feeling. They even eye each other with suspicion. And we giggle like children. Oh, such fun! I wonder if Siouxsie ever tried pissing on them?

But, alas, the third time is not a charm, and Neil finally blows the game. He lets another dash of piss slip from the glass, but fails to pull back in time, lingering a moment too long to admire his handiwork. What follows is like a scene from *Invasion Of The Bodysnatchers*, *that* scene, as a mutant Donald Sutherland points an accusing finger and lets out that horrible moan. Except this fucker looks nothing like Donald Sutherland, not least since Mr Sutherland hasn't got a shaved head and facial tattoos. Not surprisingly, he is not a happy bunny.

Joined once more by their single neuron, he and his friends all go off at once, jabbing nail-bitten digits at us and yelling insults. Well, presumably insults, possibly death threats. It's not like we can hear them above the music. A couple of them look like they're frothing at the mouth and Neil is not improving the situation by baiting them with offensive hand gestures, which, for some reason, causes them to jump up and down like dogs restrained by leashes that are just that bit too short for them to reach us. Except, of course, that they are not restrained. Which, to put it mildly, is something of a worry. All that is separating us from vicious kicking is a couple of sticky passes and a couple of large bouncers, who so far have seemed rather disinclined to stop any fights.

Neil, contrary to my earlier assessment of him as a reasonably sane human being, is oblivious to the fact that we might be in danger and continues, through the medium of mime, to suggest that the skinheads might be inclined towards onanism. But more worrying still is when the skinheads suddenly disappear from view. Where the fuck did they go? Did they simply move so as not to get splashed with more piss or are they looking for a way to get to us? Apparently unconcerned, Neil sits back in his seat to watch the band. I'm beginning to suspect that he's not right in the head.

Meanwhile, the large pack of skinheads in the middle of the dance floor has started up their "Sieg Heil" chant afresh and it's not long before there's another fight. Although, calling it a fight would be to suggest that two sides are involved. This is just some poor sod getting a kicking. Once again, the band stop playing but this time it seems to signal a premature end to the show. Siouxsie throws down her microphone and stomps off stage, and moments later the house lights come on. Another small victory for the master race in a war they can never hope to win. Indeed, a war they're too fucking stupid to know is over. A handful of them keep up their chant, possibly too dim to even be aware that the gig is over, but surprisingly the majority just filter quietly out of the building, their moronic objective achieved. We linger inside the venue for as long as possible, not entirely keen to meet them again, but they're gone by the time we get outside.

It turns out that the Banshees are doing a signing for the gaggle of fans still lurking around the building, all of the band seated behind a long table in a small room adjoining the main venue.

It's an intimate affair, remarkably cheerful and friendly considering how the show went, but perhaps also a thank you, an acknowledgement to those who endured it. Contrary to what I've heard of their reputation, the band are all smiles, possibly relieved that the night is over without anyone getting seriously hurt. I get to the front of the line and hand over a T-shirt to be signed.

"Why am I signing this?" asks Siouxsie.

"I'm following the tour," I tell her. "I can't afford one of your shirts."

And thus I have, to this day, the only Cockney Rejects shirt in the world to be signed by Siouxsie and the Banshees.

Of course, it was a lie, of sorts, that I was following the tour, this being the first gig I'd seen on the tour, and only the third Banshees show I'd ever seen. But it was also, perhaps, an unconsidered truth. Why not follow the tour, after all? It wasn't as if I had any other plans. And while Neil shows no signs of actually knowing the band, nor they him, he certainly knows someone who does. Maybe one of the road crew. We could get in for "nuffin".

Unfortunately a quick glance at the tour shirt I haven't bought tells me that the next gig is in Torquay, a place of which I know nothing other than it's where Faulty Towers is set, and possibly near the south-west pointy end of England, a long way away from Southend. Our chances of hitching there in a day are probably slim. A more pressing concern, however, is where we're going to go tonight.

The signing comes to an end and we head back outside into the night, for some reason finding ourselves loitering around the back of the venue until we figure out what to do next. The town centre isn't far away, easy walking distance, all twinkling seaside lights, but that way lies closing-time drunks and possibly large numbers of skinheads. Some of them covered in Neil's piss and not at all happy about it. Pissed off, as it were.

But we can't stay around the back of the venue all night, and after a long wait we break cover and sneak across the car park, trying to look inconspicuous. We've gone no more than about twenty yards when the cops show up, two of them appearing out of nowhere, like fucking ninjas! Christ knows where they came from or how we missed them, but they've probably been watching us for a while. Neil looks like he's about to take flight, which means I'll have to leg it too, but thankfully, he stands his ground.

"What're you doing, lads?" asks the younger of the two, in a cheery manner.

"Just been to see a band," I tell him, nodding towards the venue.

"Bit late to be hanging around out here, isn't it?" replies the young Sherlock Holmes. "The concert finished a while ago."

"We've been backstage with the band," lies Neil, flashing a pass that gives us no such access.

"So you're not stealing cars, then?" the older cop gives a false smile.

I'm not really sure what he expects us to say: "Fair cop, guv'nor. We were just about to have it away with that Escort." Although, I found out years later that a Banshees fan/roadie called Captain Scarlet was in the habit of stealing cars after every show so he could get to the next gig, so the cop wasn't too far off the mark. Instead we offer innocent smiles that say butter wouldn't melt. Well, I do. Neil, unfortunately, gives him a look that says he's about to do a runner.

"Do you want to empty your pockets?" asks the younger cop, as if we have a choice.

They split us up and we empty out assorted crap onto the front and rear of the nearest car. Neil, still acting like he's going to do a runner, gets the older one, and it suddenly occurs to me how little I know about him. What if he's got a loaded gun or half a pound of smack in his pocket? What do I *really* know about him? And what, for that matter, does he know about me? He doesn't even know my real name. Now is not a good time for nasty surprises.

The younger cop is friendly enough, although it's clear that he missed any hint of rebellion in his teenage years and has little understanding of scruffy oiks in leather jackets. Having jotted down my life history in his notebook, he sifts through the rubbish from my pockets with the end of his pen, waiting for his radio to tell him if I'm wanted for anything. He hasn't bothered to look inside my sleeping bag although all he'd find is spare T-shirts and socks, it being rather foolish to carry drugs on one's person when you look like we do. I just hope to God that Neil is not such a fool, banking on the fact that if he had any drugs we'd have taken them already.

"How was the concert?" the cop asks, attempting to make idle conversation as he empties my cigarettes from their packet, peering inside as if he's expecting to find something other than a now empty packet.

"Okay," I shrug. "Too many skinheads causing trouble."

"Yeah, we get a lot of them around here," he sympathises. "Especially at the bank holidays. Bloody nuisance…"

He trails off, distracted by his radio telling him that I'm not a wanted criminal, and Neil comes through clean on the other cop's radio, known but not wanted. We put the crap back in our pockets, cigarettes, lighters, loose change, old gig tickets…

"Where are you planning on sleeping tonight?" the older cop asks.

"Don't know yet," I confess. There seems little point in lying. Anywhere but here.

"I'd suggest you head that way," he nods away from the town centre towards a dark and distant stretch of coastline. "It's the posh end of town. You should be safe enough, so long as you keep your noses clean. Alright then, off you go."

We thank them for their time – even though it was ours – and for their useful advice, then amble off in the direction suggested, Neil muttering complaints about them wasting our time, like we had some other pressing engagement. In all likelihood they just saved us from getting a kicking. We walk at least a mile, maybe two, before deciding that we're probably far enough away from town.

The beach is silent except for the slow breaking of lazy waves, a gentle hiss as the sea creeps up to meet the shore. We sit against an upturned rowing boat, quietly smoking cigarettes. I assume we'll be sleeping here, but Neil has a better idea; he lifts the side of the boat revealing enough space for both of us. Protection in the unlikely event of rain and a hiding place from any stray boneheads. We clamber underneath into total darkness and I use my sleeping bag as a pillow rather than unroll it and have it get all sandy. There are shuffling noises as we attempt to get comfortable and then nothing but the beautiful whisper of the waves, spoiled only by the ringing in my ears from the gig. I stare into the blackness, waiting for my eyes to adjust, but there is nothing but dark. I close my eyes and stare at the inside of my eyelids, still wide awake. Neil starts snoring.

CHAPTER EIGHT

DAY BREAKS − or at least cracks a little bit – and Neil is still snoring. He's been doing it all night, horrible guttural phlegm noises, like he's gargling oysters, and I've barely got a wink of sleep. Not that this is entirely Neil's fault, much of my insomnia being induced by paranoid thoughts of roaming boneheads, but it certainly hasn't helped. No amount of elbowing him in the ribs will shut him up.

I squeeze out from under the boat into what promises to be another beautiful summer's day, dragging my sleeping bag behind me, patting myself free of sand. Neil doesn't wake up, even after I've kicked the side of the boat, so I go for a walk, heading vaguely towards town, no particular destination. I find a public toilet and wash in the freezing cold water of the sink, then dig a clean Motörhead shirt out of my bag and spend some time fixing my hair, before noticing that someone has written 'shit' almost illegibly in shit on the once-white wall. Presumably their own shit. So much for getting clean.

Outside, I find a tramp rummaging through a litter bin, his search apparently fruitless.

"You're up very early this fine morning," he grins, a gruff but educated voice.

His has the usual greasy film of the long-term homeless, but his clothing is moderately smart, a much-repaired grey suit that matches his long, combed-back hair and well-groomed beard. He seems more like the classic hobo by choice, rather than a nutter roaming the community, but it could just be that he sounds quite posh.

"What time is it?"

"Seven-ish," he shrugs, straightening himself up from the bin. "I doubt you usually rise with the sun. Couldn't sleep down there on the beach?"

"How did you know?" I ask stupidly. It's not as if Neil couldn't be heard from several miles away.

"I know everything," he replies modestly, digging some matches out of his pocket and lighting an old dog end. He manages to get a few puffs out of the wretched thing, singeing his beard in the process, before discarding it and letting out a fearsome, hacking cough. I give him one of my smokes from a crumpled packet that I seem to have been lying on all night.

"Got any money?"

"No," I lie.

"Perhaps we'd best find some, then," he grins a nicotine-stained grin. "I'm Reg," he offers a grubby hand.

I follow him back towards the seafront, stopping at every bin to look for empty bottles with a deposit on them, which is how he makes a living. He's good company, even if some of what he says seems like random gibberish, and extremely proud of the fact that he's self-sufficient and doesn't sign on or beg for money. Apparently, asking if I had any doesn't count. Somewhere along the line he just opted out of society, got sick of tax forms and working all hours for little in return. Now he lives off whatever he can find.

"What's the point," he asks rhetorically, "in choosing to have no part in society if you are going to conform to its restraints by relying on it for money?"

He then tells me that he has no fillings, which rather proves the point about random gibberish. But he's a happy soul nonetheless, content with his lot. He kind of reminds me of the local tramp, Theodore, back home. Except without the terrible stench.

Theodore has become something of a tourist attraction over the years, although I don't recall anyone treating him with much kindness, more as a conversation piece. He's fond of punk rockers, because we'll usually take time to talk to him, but he hates the music, apparently because he used to be a concert pianist long ago, before he fucked up somehow and his family disowned him. It's one of those things you don't pry about. He really stinks though, even in winter when he becomes massive from wearing so many layers of clothing, and you have to pray that the wind doesn't change direction after you've settled down for a chat. Rumour has it, the Salvation Army catches up with him once a year and disinfects him.

Almost back near the boat, Reg stops at a newsagent's, cashes in the bottles and buys himself ten No. 6. He tries to give me the rest of the change.

"You take it," he says, holding out a few coins. "Make sure you look after yourself."

"You keep it," I tell him, feeling not a little guilty for lying about having no money. It's not like I have much – some meagre savings, mostly hidden in my sock – but I have more than him. "Really, Reg, I'll be fine."

"If you're sure," he shrugs, tucking the coins into his pocket.

We part ways with another grubby handshake and he points me in the right direction for the A127 out of town, back to London. I'm tempted to go alone, leave Neil behind, but it seems a bit cuntish, so I head back to the boat, checking the gig guide as I go. Neil is still asleep, snoring like a warthog with sleep apnoea, and I have to kick the side of the boat several times before he grudgingly emerges.

"Alright, alright, keep ya fuckin' 'air on," he whines, clearly not a 'morning person'.

He clambers out from under the boat, slapping his jeans free of sand and wiping his face with his T-shirt.

"What's the plan? Where're we goin'?"

We? Obviously he thinks his company is welcome and I suppose it is. For now.

"I reckon we could make it to Bath," I tell him, pointing at my crumpled map. "Killing Joke are playing there."

"Killing Joke, yeah?" He clears his nose by blocking one nostril with his finger and firing hideous mucus from the other. "I know them. We can get in for nuffin.'"

The walk out of town seems to take hours, not least because Neil moans like an old woman, dragging his feet in the dust and kicking at stones. He wants to stop as soon as we reach the start of the A127, but it's patently a rubbish place to hitch from, not a good place for cars to stop, so I insist that we keep walking. Neil mutters something under his breath and trudges resentfully on. If he doesn't cheer up soon, I'll leave him behind. I'm used to hitching alone, setting my own pace and walking for hours if I don't get a ride. It's undoubtedly safer hitching with someone else, but you have to make compromises and you're less likely to get a ride unless your companion is female. Right now, Neil is just slowing me down.

We reach the next junction and he plonks himself on the grass verge, refusing to walk any further.

"Can't we just wait 'ere?" he whines.

I agree to rest for a while, which apparently means Neil lying on his back with his hands behind his head, while I stand by the curb with my thumb out. The sun beats down and I take my leather jacket off, trying not to appear too sweaty or obnoxious, a task made all the more difficult by Neil picking his nose. There's an art to altering your appearance so you'll get a lift easier; a few subtle changes in stance and facial expression and you become a harmless – if slightly scruffy – kid, rather than a horrible oik who's possibly wired on drugs and wanted by the police. A friendly smile will often do the trick, but my efforts are wasted when my companion is lying there in a swastika T-shirt, flicking bogies off his finger. We wait for a couple of hours before Neil reluctantly agrees to start walking again.

"I'm fuckin' thirsty," he grumbles pointlessly.

"So am I, but there's no shops."

"We could knock on the door of that 'ouse and ask for some water, yeah?" he nods at a lone house about half a mile or so ahead.

"And you really think they'll give you some?"

"They might. It's worth a try."

No, it's not. It's a retarded idea. No one in their right mind is going to open their door to a pair of suspicious-looking characters like us, much less let us into their home. Please God, I think, let us get a lift before we get to the house. But, of course, we draw closer with no sign of salvation.

"Let's just ask, yeah?" Neil insists. And before I can stop him, he disappears down a grass bank and along the short garden path.

I loiter at the top of the bank, feeling nervous. Something is going to go horribly wrong. I can see Neil peering into the windows, looking almost exactly how you'd imagine a potential burglar would look.

"'ullo?" he yells through the letterbox. "Anyone there?"

He raps on the door: "'ullo?" then turns to me: "I don't think there's no one in."

"Well, come back up here, then, for fuck's sake."

It's quite likely that he's right and there's not 'no one in'. Some poor old biddy is probably hiding in there. Just as I'm thinking that, a face appears at one of the side windows. It is indeed the face of an old woman. An extremely worried and very, very old woman, who, if she has a phone, will, without question, call the police within about the next two seconds.

"'ullo? Anyone there?" Neil persists through the letterbox, having not seen the woman.

"Look, there's obviously no one in, so you'll have to do without a drink of water," I say, hopefully loud enough for the old dear to hear.

Please, God, don't let her call the cops or die of fright! Fuck, what if she calls the cops and then dies of fright? We'll go to prison for a glass of water!

"I don't think no one lives 'ere," Neil concludes, peering again through the letterbox. "We could prob'ly get in 'round the back."

No, Neil, we couldn't! Stop being such a cunt!

Just then, a big, green van pulls up at the curb, and a man leans across the passenger seat to yell something at me. I can't hear what he's saying, but already my mind has decided that he's some have-a-go-hero who's going to wrestle us both to the ground before making a citizen's arrest. His lips move, but there's no sound above the passing traffic. And then it dawns on me, as Neil strides back up the bank and passes me, that the bloke is just trying to give us a lift.

"We're going to Bath, yeah?" Neil says, climbing into the passenger seat before the man has a chance to answer.

I climb in behind him and do the introductions, since Neil obviously has no intention of doing so, instead completely ignoring the man and flicking through a newspaper from the dashboard. But, thankfully, it seems like the bloke only picked us up so he'll have someone to talk at and I don't have to put much into the conversation. He's boring to the point of soporific, prattling on about the weather, mostly, but at least we're moving, albeit rather slowly, the van doing no more than forty miles an hour. I manage to nod in the appropriate places, while Neil continues to ignore him. Eventually he drops us off at the start of the M4 motorway.

There's a handful of hitchhikers here already, most of whom are obviously going to get rides before us, even if it weren't for the unspoken first-come-first-served etiquette of hitching. Nice, smart student types with neatly printed signs reading 'Wales please', a truck driver with one of those red number plates… Hell, even the lone hippie at the end of the line looks vaguely like a member of the human race and not some horrible guttersnipe who's been sleeping under a boat.

This could call for some serious patience and the fact that Neil has none drains mine considerably. He adopts his ever-helpful look of total apathy, curious only about the contents of his nostrils, while I struggle to look appealing. We could be in for a very long wait.

Hours pass.

The other hitchhikers get rides and more show up, some of those late-comers getting picked up instead of us, apologetic smiles as they climb into passenger seats.

"We should do a sign, yeah?" Neil suggests, from his now familiar position of being sprawled across the grass with his hands behind his head.

"Or you could get out of sight of the road." Obviously, I'm dealing with an expert here, as sitting on your arse, wearing a swastika T-shirt and picking your nose are essential to hitchhiking.

"No, we should do a sign," Neil persists.

"Have you got a pen?"

"No."

"Paper?"

"No."

"Well, shut up then."

Neil is silent for a moment, perhaps contemplating whether or not to eat what he's just picked out of his nose. He wipes the offending, and indeed offensive, item on his jeans, clambers to his feet and stomps off towards the motorway. I feel fleetingly guilty for driving him away with my foul temper, but I can't help it. He really is a cunt sometimes.

But Neil is far too thick-skinned to be put out by anything less than direct insults or physical violence. A few minutes later, he's back with a rancid and pathetically dog-eared piece of cardboard that has doubtless been employed by several generations of hitchhikers before he found it. In scrappy letters, bordering on illiteracy, it bears the legend 'Bath please!'.

It takes little less than a minute for the abuse to start, and from then on it's pretty much constant. People actually slow down just to take the piss, and having gone to such enormous effort to get us a sign, Neil doesn't find this remotely amusing. He yells abuse back at them, spits at their cars, and even takes a swing at one of the slower moving vehicles with his boot. Quite how he fails to see the funny side is beyond me: Two dirty punk rockers with a sign that says 'Bath please!' How is that not funny? But apparently Neil doesn't think so.

After another hour of increasingly less witty comments, however, I'm beginning to see his point. We're not going anywhere, and Bath is still a long way away. Worse still, all of the first hitchhikers have been picked up and most of the new batch have gone, too. We're the last turkeys in the shop, the strays that no one wants.

"This is bollocks," moans Neil, plonking himself back on the grass. "Ain't there any gigs in London?"

"Nothing decent, but we might have to give up soon," I concede. "We'll give it another ten minutes, yeah?" I add, kicking myself for picking up his "yeah?" habit.

Ten minutes pass. Fifteen. I hate giving up, but there seems little choice.

And then, as if by magic, a red hatchback pulls into the curb, with a trendy-looking couple in the front. The woman leans out of the already open window.

"Are you going to see Killing Joke?" she smiles.

We both nod like idiots as she motions us to get in the car.

"We're doing their merch," she says. "We can take you right to the venue."

There is a God! All this time, I've been questioning the existence of some all-seeing, omnipotent being, and yet here she is, handing us cigarettes from the front seat of a hatchback. I see now the error of my ways, and why Mr Blunden was right for suggesting, on my school report, that I had no moral values because I had, at the tender age of eleven, rejected religion. God gives us a light and then lights a cigarette for her driver. She puts on a Stranglers tape and we sit back to enjoy the ride, windows down, the warm breeze buffeting our faces.

Immediately, Neil becomes more animated and conversational; there's something to gain here, even if it's just a free T-shirt. It's amusing watching him angle for whatever he can get, but I'm quite pleased that God isn't taking the bait. We do smoke all of her cigarettes, though, and have to make a stop at the services for another pack.

We all step out of the car to stretch our legs and take a piss, and I dip back in to get my jacket, more out of habit than the fear that it's going to get stolen. Under the jacket is a huge burn mark that definitely wasn't there when we got in. Oh Christ, I've set fire to God's car! A few miles back, I flicked a butt out of the window and it seemed to get blown back in. I said nothing at the time, surreptitiously shifting around to find it before deciding that it must have gone out of the window after all. But here, under my jacket, is a burn mark the size of my hand, and the small, brown butt of evidence. I cover it temporarily with my sleeping bag, while the couple make me feel even more guilty by paying for coffee. I say nothing when we pull away, but I don't smoke any more of God's cigarettes.

If you happen to be reading this now, God, I'm very sorry.

CHAPTER NINE

IN BATH, WE circle a few times looking for the venue, before getting the right directions. It's a magnificent city with a history that dates back to pre-Roman times, and Bath Pavilion, although built considerably later, is no less impressive. A sandstone, Edwardian period building, constructed in 1910 and designed to be 'Bath's premium venue for recreation and entertainment', it sits close to the Bath Rugby Football Club, a stone's throw from the River Avon. A look now at Google Maps suggests that nothing much has changed. It's a truly beautiful city and I wish that I'd taken some time to look around it properly, or been old enough to appreciate it.

Departing the car, I slyly cover the burn mark with a newspaper from the back window ledge. We thank the couple for the ride and I follow Neil to the back of the venue where he disappears to sort out free tickets again. This time he's back almost immediately, wearing the now familiar something-for-nothing grin. Remarkably, he's accompanied by Killing Joke's bassist, Youth, who chats with us for a while and is a thoroughly nice bloke, even though I'm a bit star-struck and probably said something stupid.

On a patch of grass over by the shimmering river, there is a group of a dozen or more punks, relaxing in the hot sun and drinking cider. Neil and I wander over to join them, and a grubby-looking, blue-haired youth, in a particularly scabby jacket, hands us his bottle. The cider is warm and we both wipe the top of the bottle in case he's got something contagious, but we drink gratefully. No one really bothers with introductions, except Dog, whose cider we are drinking, but everyone is friendly. About half of them are from Bristol, two are from Plymouth, and the rest are local. The two from Plymouth are telling horror stories about hitching here, how they were dropped in the middle of nowhere a couple of times and chased by football fans. It's nothing out of the ordinary, but they make the tale entertaining.

Neil suggests that we go and acquire some alcohol, but I don't really feel like going anywhere, especially since he probably plans to steal said alcohol and I don't fancy getting caught shoplifting. Instead, I give him some change and tell him to get me a bottle of cider, which inevitably means that he'll keep the money and steal the cider. Not that I really care. At least it means I don't have to go anywhere.

It's nice here by the river, and the company is relaxed and good-natured. We talk and smile, share cigarettes and cider like old friends, even though we've only just met. The sun beats down, giving even Dog a healthy glow under all that grime. Someone suggests that we go swimming, but while the water winks invitingly no one is sure how clean it is. It's not like the Roman spas that Bath is so famous for; there could be anything lurking beneath that enticingly cool surface; shopping carts, bicycles, dead rats, used johnnies, human excrement... Even Dog – who has a thick, black tidemark around his neck and bears more than a passing resemblance to Pigpen from the Charlie Brown cartoons – goes off the idea of taking a dip. And as tempting as it is to throw him in, no one wants to disrupt the peace.

A couple more punks join the group and the conversation breaks from one bunch, all telling stories and jokes, to smaller conversations between twos and threes. We're still all together, but the exchanges become more intimate, Dog and I telling increasingly exaggerated stories of hitchhiking, most of them lies, while on the other side of our loose circle the Bristol punks trade filthy jokes. A punk girl joins Dog and I, sitting to my right, and Dog hands her a freshly opened but warm bottle of cider. She drinks thirstily, hands me the bottle, and introduces herself as Beki.

She's pretty, with long, black, spiky hair trailing down into rats' tails that reach her pale shoulders and the torn collar of a much-worn Killing Joke T-shirt. Her green eyes sparkle like the river, and every time she leans forward I get a glimpse of her dark, pert nipple, where she's cut the sleeves off the shirt and the sides hang low. She catches me looking and gives me a warm, flirtatious smile as I look away. Dog is still telling the tale of taking three days to hitch to Sunderland in the pissing rain, but somehow I'm not really listening anymore. Beki leans forward again for no apparent reason other than to tease, and, rather slow on the uptake, I realise she's doing it on purpose.

Eventually Dog seems to take the hint and clambers to his feet, saying he's going for a slash, and leaving Beki and I to our coquetry. Our talk is of bands – we both like the Damned and even went to a couple of the same shows – but our body language has nothing to do with music. We inch closer together, until finally my hand brushes against a fishnet-stockinged knee that peaks from a tear in her army combat trousers. We kiss.

A short while later, Dog returns with a punk he's just met, and they sit on the edge of our ever-increasing circle. He offers his cider around, but the bottle looks suspiciously full since he went for a piss, so we decline. Luckily, Neil chooses this moment to reappear with a couple of bottles of fortified wine, handing me one as he sits down. He then produces a carton of cigarettes from the lining of his jacket, gives me a pack, keeps two for himself, and sets about selling the rest for half price. Thieving cunt.

And so afternoon turns into early evening, the sun slowly sliding west towards the horizon, but clearly not ready to call it a night yet. Beki rests her head against my chest, careful not to mess up her hair, and we watch as a couple of the Bristol punks set about playful wrestling, possibly intent on throwing one another in the river, which was bound to happen sooner or later. It's a world away from the skinheads play-fighting in St James's Park, friendly and harmless, funny rather than frightening. No threat of imminent violence.

And then, suddenly, the sun disappears behind a cloud.

The Bristol punks cease their horseplay, frozen in position, and it's then that I realize the sky is still cloudless. Directly behind us stands a wall of nefarious-looking thugs, the biggest of which is standing at the front of the pack, right behind where Beki and I are sitting. She breaks contact with me and the spell is broken, the magic gone. He's fucking huge!

"We're the Bath Warriors!" he announces with a West Country accent so thick you could stand a spoon in it, "and we challenge your mob!"

There is silence, just the inappropriate tweeting of a nearby songbird. Nobody moves.

"We ain't really got a mob," says one of the Bristol punks, almost apologetically. "We're all from different places, like."

The gorilla is momentarily bemused, his eyebrows knitting together as if discussing what to do next. One of the Bristol punks has subtly turned his bottle around and looks ready to take them on, and the Plymouth punks look ready to run, but I can't tell much else because of the glare of the sun, and I can't risk getting to my feet yet. Even though we outnumber them, probably two-to-one, the gorillas have the clear advantage. They've chosen their position well and we have to squint into the sun to see them. And, well, they're fucking huge! Grown men. Heads like medicine balls. Arms like tree-trunks. Hands like shovels.

"Alright," the lead gorilla says slowly, "we challenge you anyway. Where are you from?" he snarls at me.

Fuck. Why me?

My mind flicks quickly through the conditioned responses and bravely settles on cowardice. Now is not the time for heroics. Particularly since there is nothing heroic about getting your face punched in, if it can be avoided.

"The Isle of Wight," I tell him, shifting just a fraction to indicate that I'm with my girlfriend and don't want any trouble. From where he's standing he could easily kick me in the face.

"Alright," he sneers, "We challenge the Isle of Wight mob!"

"Um, there's only me," I say meekly.

For a second I think he's going to hit me anyway, but he's losing momentum and he knows it, even if he's not sure why.

"Alright," he tries to regain authority, "where are *you* from?"

"London," says Neil.

"Ah," says the gorilla, on firmer ground. "Alright then, we challenge the London mob!"

"I'm on my own, sorry," says Neil, as if he's genuinely trying to be helpful.

"What about you?"

"Oxford."

The gorilla looks at his feet, sighs, and his apes shuffle uncomfortably behind him. They hadn't bargained for this. They look stupid and they know it. And there are too many girls here. From a distance all these punks look the same; dirty fucking scum who never do an honest day's work and go around slagging off the Queen. Up close though, at least half of them are birds, and you don't just go steaming into birds.

The moment drags on, silent but for the incessant tweeting of that other damn bird, its merry song as out of place as someone whistling at a funeral. Growing restless, one of the Bath Warriors clears his throat, and the lead gorilla demands a place of origin from one of the Bristol punks, who despite an equally thick West Country accent, insists that he's from Huddersfield. No two people have claimed to be from the same place.

The gorilla clenches his fists and his knuckles make a nasty cracking sound, but he's completely run out of steam and it seems unlikely that they'll attack us now. Unfortunately, that doesn't preclude him from giving me a smack in the face, just to let everyone know they've won, and simply because I'm the nearest at hand. Or possibly boot. He moves his weight from one leg to the other and, almost distractedly, draws a shape in the dust with his foot. I flinch, waiting for the inevitable blow. But it never comes. Instead, he seems to come to a decision.

"Alright," he growls. "We'll fucking get you lot later! We'll get the fucking lot of you!"

He turns and stomps away, his apes reluctantly following. From what I can make out against the glare of the sun, they look confused and not a little disappointed, but he's the leader so they follow. He turns one more as they walk away, jabbing a finger in our direction: "Just you wait! We'll 'ave you, you cunts!"

For a few moments there is quiet as we watch them go, like everyone's holding their breath, and then one of the Bristol punks starts laughing and sets the rest of us off. Mostly, it's relief that we didn't get the shit kicked out of us, but then again, with the benefit of some distance, it was very funny. Bath Warriors, for fuck's sake! What pond did these cunts crawl out of?

"Wankers," snorts Dog. "Did you see the look on their faces? They're all 'duh, we challenge your mob!'"

"I'm from 'uddersfield," grins the Bristol punk.

"I'm French!" says another. "Why do you think I have this outrageous accent?"

"I'm Brian and so's my wife!"

Everyone hoots with laughter and Beki moves a little closer again, holds my hand. Dog does an impression of the lead gorilla, frowning until he's almost cross-eyed and puffing his shoulders out. It's not very good but we all laugh anyway. I take a generous swig of wine and hand the bottle to Beki, then turn to Neil to crack a joke. His face is uncharacteristically sullen, eyes cold as he gulps dejectedly on his wine.

"Wass the matter with you?" I slur slightly, pissed again now that the the fear has passed.

He lets out a sigh, lights himself a cigarette. He looks fucking miserable.

"Y'know when I went to get the wine, yeah?"

"Yeah."

"Well, I had a quick nose about inside the venue, too. The Bath Warriors are the bouncers tonight. We're gonna get killed."

CHAPTER TEN

THE SUN DIPS its head as if sensing our mood, our Eden destroyed, paradise very much lost. With the knowledge of what we may face tonight, all jokes fall flat. No one is funny anymore. A swarm of gnats has moved upriver to feast on our bare arms and necks. And not that it was ever good, but suddenly this wine tastes disgusting.

Our circle depletes, people drifting away, most without saying goodbye. News that the Bath Warriors are the bouncers for tonight's show has put such a damper on everyone's spirits that they may as well have attacked us physically, just to get it done with. Not that we'd have stood a chance of winning, but we may at least have shown some semblance of loyalty. The Bristol punks would have stuck together, as they doubtless still will in the event of trouble, but the rest of us are on our own. If it comes down to it, I know Neil won't back me up against those monsters, nor I him. We certainly won't fight for people we don't know.

Eventually we climb to our feet, drowsy and drunk from sun and wine. Neil treads out his cigarette and we amble wearily towards the venue and certain doom. As crazy as it may sound, turning away and missing the gig is not an option, not even mentioned. All gigs come with a high possibility of violence, it's just that in this case we've been forewarned. To this day, I don't know if it was bravery or stupidity that made us continue going to gigs at all.

Neil and I manage to avoid running the gauntlet of Bath Warriors on the main door by going to the guest entrance and then to the cloakroom to drop off my sleeping bag. But as we meet up with Beki in the foyer, a couple of them shoulder their way through the crowd past us. One of them takes a second look, a brief glimmer of recognition dimly lighting his face. With any luck, their mind-boggling stupidity could be our redemption. Any more brainless and they'd have trouble recognising each other at the start of each new shift. Which, I suppose, makes the job more interesting.

"Alright, Dave. I see we've got another new doorman tonight."

"Oh yeah. Who's that?"

"Who's who?"

"New doorman."

"Are ya? 'ow do ya do? My name's Dave…"

Neil disappears into the main venue to ponce some money or steal something or whatever it is he does in the shadows, and I head to the bar with Beki. There's a handful of skinheads in there, hunched around a couple of tables, looking furtive, but they're not causing any trouble, perhaps too few in number or too wary of the bouncers to start any shit. Maybe they're not the troublemaking kind, but we give them a wide berth just in case. I get a couple of pints and we head back out through the growing throng into the darkened hall, the shadows and noise disguising the fact that our conversation has dried up.

Beki is seventeen and lives here in Bath with her parents, which is bad news because it means it's unlikely that Neil and I will be able to crash at her place. There's always room in a squat, maybe even a bed if you're lucky, but parents generally don't take too kindly to unwashed punks showing up on their doorstep at midnight with their innocent young daughter. Even if they're not so innocent.

We finish our pints as the opening band, Talisman, start their set, thick reggae beats pulsing from the stage. Beki decides that this would be a great moment to stick her tongue down my throat. Regrettably, my stomach decides that it would rather remind me that it's had nothing but cider and wine for two days and really isn't happy about it. There's a sudden wave of nausea and my mouth does that horrible watering thing that comes before throwing up. I need air, cool night air, but doubtless there's a no readmission policy and I'm not about to discuss it with the Bath Warriors, who are unlikely, I suspect, to be entirely sympathetic.

I lean heavily against the wall, which is damp and chilled with condensation from the heat of the venue. I swallow hard, trying to keep from puking, eyes closed, breathing like a dying fish, my T-shirt soaked in sweat as I boil over like a car stuck in bank holiday traffic. I must have air!

Beki puts a supportive arm around me, wisely managing to keep her distance in case I throw up, and I swallow again, mumbling that I'll be alright in a minute. And then another wave of nausea… I push Beki aside and rush toward the toilets, my vision blurred, gait uncontrolled, like my legs want to go in different directions. All I can think is, please, God, don't let me puke on any skinheads or bouncers.

I make it to the toilet and collapse over the sink with my head pressed against the cool porcelain. Deep breaths. I splash cold water on my face, still fighting to keep the contents of my stomach where they are. In the cracked and dirty mirror, my skin is drenched with sweat and seems to have gone a terrible grey/green colour. More deep breaths. More water. Slowly the nausea passes, but I cling to the sink like it's a life raft, unsure of my treacherous legs.

It's then, rather surprisingly, that I hear someone call my name in a thick West Country accent. The accent's not surprising, obviously, since everyone talks like that around here, but no one knows my name. I look around, and there in the doorway, indeed taking up the entire doorway, is the biggest skinhead I've ever seen. Surprise turns to shock. He fills the space more completely than if it had been bricked up. The fucker is huge!

"You Morat?" he demands again.

I nod, utterly terrified. How the fuck does he know my name?

"My bird wants to talk to you."

I nod again, like a prisoner quietly acknowledging a death sentence, and resignedly follow him to the foyer. It's not like I have a choice. It's not like this makes any sense. I don't know him, never met him, and have no idea what's going on, although various scenarios play through my head, all of them bad. Perhaps this will be one of those ridiculous "you shagged my bird" situations, where I'll be confronted by an aggressive tomboy who I've never so much as laid eyes on, and then be forced to make pointless denials. Or maybe she's just going to hit me, knowing full well that if I retaliate then her leviathan boyfriend will stamp on my head as carelessly as a child through puddles. I simply have no idea.

The main doors are open and a cool breeze strokes my sodden brow as we pass. My vision is still blurred, but there can be no doubt, as we reach the centre of the foyer, that the skinhead's bird is standing in front of me, smiling, vaguely expectant. She has blonde, spiky hair, and is clad in a studded leather jacket, tartan miniskirt, and one of those expensive cheesecloth bondage shirts. She also carries a battered, old lady's handbag, possibly having battered an old lady to get it. I try to focus on her face, pretty if it wasn't so sharp, but for a moment she has two heads and I have to stare at her heavily-pierced ear to stop the room from spinning. I still have no idea who the fuck she is.

"Oi thought it was you," she enthuses, with the same yokel accent as her frightening lover. "Oi saw your jacket when you went in the bogs."

I have a distinctive Damned logo on the back of my jacket, but the fact that she recognises it offers me no further clues to her identity.

"It's Sue," she adds helpfully, noting my blank expression. "Sue from Bath."

Still a complete fucking blank. The strain is unbearable; I'm bad with names and faces at the best of times – either drunk when I meet people or not paying attention because I don't expect to ever see them again – but to be faced with someone I'm certain I've never met before, someone who clearly thinks we're friends, is simply too much to deal with in this addled state. Particularly with her terrifying boyfriend lurking beside her, ready at any moment to pull my arms from their sockets and beat me to death with the soggy ends if I displease her. The only sensible option is to lie.

"Fucking hell, Sue!" I slur hopelessly. "'s good to see you! How's it going?"

This seems to do the trick.

"Jane's gone all trendy," she informs, as if conveying the news of a death in the family. "All that New Romantic crap…"

I mutter my condolences.

And then it suddenly dawns on me…

Sue and Jane were among the handful of penfriends I wrote to for a few months, before I got bored with it and the letters fizzled out. It's what we did in the old days, pre-internet. There would be adverts in the personals section of *Sounds* magazine, and one would write a letter – including a photograph – to anyone who seemed vaguely interesting – i.e. liked the same bands as you, or might possibly take their knickers off for you. If you were lucky, you'd get a response through the post a couple of weeks later. Let's just say that Tinder and dick pics were still a long way off.

Looking back, there was almost certainly some kind of adolescent fantasy involved, but I never actually expected to meet any of them. And, of course, once faced with one of my largely illiterate acquaintances, I had very little to say. I'd forgotten the contents of every one of her letters and knew nothing about her except, with quite reasonable certainty, that I had no desire whatsoever to spend the night with her.

Admittedly, things might have been different were she not accompanied by a gigantic caveman, but he clearly intended to cause great bodily harm to anyone who so much as spoke to the apple of his eye uninvited, much less tried to pluck her. This situation called for a great deal of tact, a detailed recollection of her written offerings – I'm pretty sure I'd remember if she'd mentioned an enormous skinhead – and, most of all, a silver tongue. Alas, right now, I possess none of these gifts. I can barely stand up.

"Bath Warriors," I blurt drunkenly. "They're gonna kill me!"

Clearly aware of who I'm talking about, Sue looks towards the bouncers at the main doors, and then back at me. She lights a cigarette from her handbag, passes it to the waiting mouth of her boyfriend, like a small bird feeding an overgrown cuckoo. He did say she was his bird. Presumably not allowed matches, he takes a puff on the cigarette and slowly shifts his gaze from Sue to the bouncers, then back to her. She smiles a rather unnerving smile.

"Oh, don't you worry about them," she tells me, as if dealing with a small child who's grazed his knee. "You get any shit from them and you tell 'em you're with Big Kev. You get any shit from *anyone* and you tell 'em you with Big Kev."

I look up at Big Kev – Lurch with a shaved head – and he looks back, nodding contentedly at the prospect of hurting someone. He grins at me, trying to be friendly, looking not unlike a bulldog chewing a wasp.

"Everyone's scared of Big Kev," Sue continues proudly. "He bit someone's nose off, once."

He could hardly bite someone's nose off twice.

Big Kev grins down at me again, relishing those fond memories; chewing them over, so to speak. It's then that I notice that everyone who walks through the foyer gives him an extremely wide berth, like there's some invisible force field around him. No one so much as stands in his shadow. Big Kev rules his domain, the king of the skinheads, while Sue, with her crown of blonde spikes, plays the evil queen. Apparently I have become their jester.

Finding myself rapidly more sober in such company, I make small talk with the happy couple, blindly agreeing with everything they say, and hoping to God that they never reproduce. Christ, what a terrible mutant that would be! No brain, just a thick skull for headbutting people. Knuckles dragging along the ground. A boy would be even worse!

As tactfully as possible, I disengage myself from the conversation, if you could call it such, and, promising faithfully to write to Sue as soon as the opportunity arises, I hurry back to the main hall.

"Don't forget," Sue calls for everyone to hear, "you get any shit off anyone and you tell 'em Big Kev'll flatten 'em!"

Considerably more sober, and with the fresh swagger in my step that comes with being untouchable, I head to the bar. Having located a neglected pint, I search briefly for Beki and find her not quite so neglected. In fact, she has moved only a couple of feet, but presently has her lips suctioned to the face of a punk with a blue Mohican, huge, purple love bites covering her neck. So much for young love. I should get Big Kev to flatten him.

CHAPTER ELEVEN

WITH THE ROYAL seal of approval, I am free to wander the venue unthreatened. It's an unusual feeling, I suppose like having a big brother, and one to which I could happily become accustomed. Evidently, word has got around that I am to be left alone, and I find myself standing amid a small gang of skinheads without getting so much as a dirty look. One of them even gives me a nod of acknowledgement.

To be fair, they could be the fabled skins I've heard about who don't go around looking for trouble, but I'm not about to take any chances with them, so I move away. Aside from the bouncers there's been no threat of violence tonight and the atmosphere is pleasantly cordial, the Killing Joke vibe. But, of course, as soon as that thought crosses my mind, there's a scuffle in the darkness, over by the far wall. A punk with a blue Mohican is throwing punches and haphazardly aiming his boot at another punk, while a girl tries to get between them and pull them apart: Beki is having her honour fought for, such as it is. The fight fizzles out like a damp sparkler.

The laid-back atmosphere, however, is conducive to watching the band alone, and while it occurs to me that I haven't seen Neil for at least an hour, it's nice to be able to get lost in music without him badgering me for cigarettes or whatever, talking through all the songs. The likes of *Wardance* and *Pssyche* tend to lose much of their potency when someone won't shut up, but for the next hour or so I am left in peace to watch another awesome performance.

Towards the end of the set, I slip away to gather my possessions from the cloakroom, then watch the encore from the back of the hall, ready to leave as soon as the show is over. I still haven't seen Neil and I have nowhere to go, but it is not lost on me that it might be a bad idea hanging around after Big Kev has gone home to his mum's house or the secure ward of the local nuthouse, wherever he rests his ugly head. I light a cigarette and Neil suddenly appears at my side, like he's got a built-in nicotine radar. He has his own cigarettes, but apparently mine taste better.

"Alright, yeah?" he beams, helping himself to a smoke.

"Yeah. What's the plan?"

He shrugs: "Dunno, but I heard the boneheads patrol the town all night kicking the shit out of anything that moves."

"What if we stay still?"

"Huh?"

"Nothing. What are we gonna do?"

"Wait here," Neil instructs, disappearing in the direction of the merch booth. He's back before the end of the last song. "We're goin' to London, yeah?"

The merchandise people who so kindly gave us a lift here are understandably reluctant to give us a lift back, but Neil's relentless pestering has left them little choice. He conveniently vanishes while I help them load their wares into the car, reappearing moments later, like some grubby little wizard. They will probably never pick up another hitchhiker as long as they live, particularly when they find the burn mark that I so discreetly covered this afternoon.

The unfortunate couple's ordeal is made worse by the fact that we are both drunk. Neil jabbers away non-stop, barely pausing for breath, full-on bullshit mode, while I stare vacantly at the passing darkness, trying not to throw up, then frantically wind the window down, sucking in the night air and making occasional retching noises. Oh what joyous company we must make.

Neil does his best throughout the journey to persuade our friends that it would be a good idea to put us up for the night – we wouldn't take up much space, a bit of floor would do – but even I'm not convinced. He has become increasingly animated, to the point where he's shouting almost constantly, possibly on speed, and I have made several more retching noises, although, as yet, I've failed to redecorate the side of their car. Not surprisingly, they want to get rid of us as soon as possible.

Finally, we draw to a halt and I tumble out onto the pavement, vomiting its breadth like a fire extinguisher going off. Bent double, with my hands on my knees, I spray froth and alcohol from my nose and mouth, tears streaming down my face. I can't see much more than a blur of street lights and passing cars, but I can hear Neil aggressively arguing with the driver about something.

"You're a cunt, you know that?" he bellows ungratefully, aiming a boot at the back of the car as it pulls away.

Standing up straight, I take in deep lungfuls of air, beautiful, dirty, city air, and wipe my face on my T-shirt, spitting out the last of my stomach lining. Neil's silhouette is on the pavement up ahead, already trying to ponce money from an obvious tourist. Beyond him is the end of Bayswater Road, Marble Arch, and the lights at the west end of Oxford Street, winking at me like a dog with a runny eye. We're back in London.

The nausea returns and against all probability I give the pavement another hosing. I'm pretty sure I didn't drink this much, and it shouldn't be possible to throw up more than you've consumed, but evidently this message has not reached my stomach. Even Neil seems mildly concerned about my welfare, momentarily leaving the tourists alone to check if I'm okay.

"You alright, yeah?"

"No."

Which appears to be the full extent of his medical expertise. He lights a cigarette, bored and impatient. Whatever nefarious activity he has in mind for the night probably didn't involve standing around watching me throw up, but it's not like I'm doing it on purpose or enjoying it.

But wait, the green-haired doctor has medicine! He produces a half bottle of vodka that he's made no previous reference to – like where the fuck he got it – and I use a small amount as mouthwash before knocking back a shot. It's cheap shit and burns all the way down, doubtless destroying what remains of my stomach lining, but against all reason it makes me feel a lot better. Thus refreshed, I am ready to see what the city has to offer.

We walk up towards Oxford Street, no particular place to go, and aimlessly turn right on Park Lane, of which I then knew nothing other than its placement on a Monopoly board and the fact that you really don't want to land there if some bastard has a hotel on it. I must confess to being somewhat in awe of its opulence, the flashy cars, red carpets, and, yes, the expensive hotels. It was another world, and one in which we stood out like aliens from some filthy, poverty-stricken planet.

From the pavement we get glimpses into this world, past immaculately-dressed doormen and beyond into foyers full of crystal chandeliers and fur coats, people spending more on one night in a hotel than I could hope to earn in a year or more. Neil flobs something brown and unpleasant onto one of the red carpets, from which it will have to be scraped before some rich fucker can stand, slide, or stick in it. More likely, the carpet will have to be humanely destroyed.

Another tourist, complete with large, highly visible camera and stupid hat, steps aside as we approach. There are hundreds of them, far more than I'd expect considering it must be about one o'clock in the morning, and Union Jack flags everywhere. But I've never been here before, so perhaps this is normal. I ask Neil, but he just shrugs a disinterested "dunno". Apparently this is not good poncing ground.

With Hyde Park to our right, we pass more expensive hotels, The Dorchester, The Park Lane Hilton, and then cross the busy street at the bottom, left onto Grosvenor Place. On the east side there is a high, barbed-wire-topped wall, that I discover many years later marks the grounds of Buckingham Palace Gardens, and on the other side are tall buildings, maybe embassies, exclusive residences and hotels. The traffic is constant, but there are no pedestrians, just us two.

For a brief moment there is a lull in the traffic, and completely without warning Neil clambers over some railings, up a drainpipe like the proverbial rat, and begins unfastening a beach towel-sized Union Flag from its pole. Astonished, I stand on the wide pavement, looking up at him, quietly freaking out. What the hell does he think he's doing? For fuck's sake, if we don't get done for attempted burglary, there's probably some archaic treason law that'll have us locked away forever for stealing national flags from halfway up extremely large buildings! It's not like we're on some hidden side street, this is clearly a major thoroughfare in a very posh part of town. Oh fuck, oh fuck, oh fuck!

"Come down, you cunt!" I hiss at him, trying not to look suspicious, like I'm not playing lookout for the stupid bastard.

The traffic builds up again, cars and trucks drifting past into the night, apparently without noticing anything untoward, but doing little to calm my nerves. A passing police car would not be so unobservant and one could happen by at any moment. Meanwhile, Neil is having some trouble unfastening the flag and is hanging precariously from the flagpole so he can get to it.

I glance up and down the street for cops, ready to leg it and leave him there. Suddenly, there's a loud flumping noise as a weighty red, white and blue standard lands at my feet. I look up, cursing, only to see our light-fingered hero struggling to free his jacket from the flagpole, wriggling and squirming like a foul-mouthed fly caught in a web. Oh glorious! Now I'm down here with the evidence, our worthless loot, while Ronnie fucking Biggs dangles up there, stuck halfway up a fucking building!

"Take your jacket off!" I yell, as another newspaper truck thunders past, praying we don't end up on the news ourselves.

Neil writhes and wriggles some more, managing to tear a hole in the arse of his jeans, but he remains firmly stuck, while I work myself into a lather of panic. What do I do? Run? Call the fire brigade to get him down? Both?

In answer to my question there is another ripping sound, and as quickly as he got up the building, Neil is back down again. He lands out of sight, behind some railings that he was lucky not to impale himself on, and I hear a groan and an irritable "bollocks" to assure me that Neil is in as good a state of health as he is ever likely to be. Climbing onto the fence, I lean over to see him lying flat on his back.

"Is the vodka alright?" I whisper, somewhat pointlessly.

"Yeah, I think so."

"Good. Now, let's get the fuck away from here!"

Neil clambers over the railings, takes the flag and ties it around his waist like a sarong, evidently not concerned with hiding the evidence, and slowly we amble away from the scene of the crime. Neil's crime; he fucking did it!

With infuriating nonchalance he hands me the unbroken vodka bottle.

"What did you steal it for?" I whine, still not entirely convinced that we won't get arrested.

He shrugs and lifts the flag to reveal the tear in his jeans: "To cover the hole in my arse."

Which wasn't there before he stole it. Cunt.

CHAPTER TWELVE

THE MAIN STREETS of Victoria are not, by any stretch of the imagination, attractive, and seem to have grown uglier with age, all dirty concrete and steel, grey, depressing, and miserably overcrowded. In the 19th century it was the site of a notorious slum called Devil's Acre, a hotbed of crime and disease, where population density was measured not by people per acre, but by people per room. Much of it was demolished to make way for what is now Victoria Street, but every year the place seems to edge a little closer to its former self. Once a shithole, always a shithole, it would seem. Even the public art is vile.

There was a venue, however, imaginatively named The Venue, at 160-162 Victoria Street, where they'd put on some legendary bands – the Ramones, the Cramps, Iggy Pop – and it's here that Neil and I find ourselves on that hot summer night, just passing by as we aimlessly wander these busy streets, polishing off the last of the vodka. I glance inside and happen to spot a very familiar face in the lobby.

"Fuckin' hell! It's Lemmy!"

"Who?"

"Lemmy from Motörhead!"

Neil shrugs, completely disinterested. But it's not like we're in a hurry to go anywhere. And even if we were, it would have to wait.

I recall that memory with great fondness, and not a little wonder at the fact that only a few years later Lemmy and I began a friendship that lasted over 30 years. Perhaps a story for another time. It certainly wasn't something I could ever have imagined as I strolled into the lobby that night, intent of getting my rather grubby *Ace Of Spades* shirt signed.

What I imagined, in fact, just moments after stepping into the lobby, was that I was probably going to get the shit kicked out of me. There were a couple of Hells Angels lurking near Lemmy, and the bouncers eyed me with great suspicion, a skinny little guttersnipe, with vomit-splashed boots, who clearly had no business being there.

Moments later, I was standing next to Lemmy, grinning like an imbecile. Me, not him, obviously.

"Alright?" he growls amiably.

No, not really. Horribly drunk, I'm suddenly aware of the heat pumping out of the club, a wall of stale, dry air that hits me like getting rugby tackled by a mattress. I start to sweat, nausea rising once more. One of the bouncers walks over to throw me out.

"No, leave him, he's alright," instructs Lemmy, and the bouncer resumes his post at the door.

"Drink this, you look like you need it."

Lemmy hands me a heavily iced drink. It looks like Ribena, tastes like fucking Ribena, except there's a weighty kick of something alcoholic in the aftertaste.

"Thanks," I manage gratefully as Lemmy lights us each a Marlboro. "Would you mind signing my shirt?"

"Sure. You got a pen?"

I sag visibly. No, I haven't got a pen. Of course I haven't got a fucking pen. Do I look like I've got a fucking pen?

"Wait here."

And with that, Lemmy disappears into the club, leaving me in the lobby with his drink.

I wait for what seems like an eternity. It's probably only about ten minutes, but it's long enough for the bouncer to start eyeing me again, possibly having forgotten that he was told not to harm me. I can see Neil loitering outside, ready and without doubt willing, to take flight without me. To be fair, I'd run away if he was getting a kicking from the bouncers.

I finish the cigarette. Lemmy's not coming back. Of course he's not coming back. Why the fuck would he?

And then he does, marker pen in hand, to scribble something illegible on my shirt. To this day I can't think of anyone else who would go to so much trouble for a fan.

"Finish it," he says, when I try to hand his drink back.

I down it in one and cheekily hand the empty glass to the bouncer on my way out.

Curious, I have scoured the internet trying to find out who was playing at the Venue that night, but with no luck. There are pictures of the place, much as I remember it, a once quite grand building, first opened as the Metropole cinema in 1929, but it's gone now, demolished in 2013 to make way for more grey ugliness.

Neil is waiting when I get outside, looking, as always, like he's up to no good. He looks suspicious even when he's standing still, but, strangely, he blends in to his surroundings a little better with the Union Jack around his waist. There are hundreds of them around here, hanging in every window, dangling from every available pole. I decide that I need one and try to persuade Neil to give me his or at least steal another one, but he's having none of it. Although, in fairness, there are a lot of people around, a party atmosphere almost, and he'd definitely get caught if he tried his little stunt again.

Still with nowhere to go, we find ourselves in Victoria station, the concourse crowded with yet more flag-waving tourists. Well, perhaps not waving, but certainly there are a lot of Union Jack hats, bags, T-shirts and such. Knowing a good thing when he sees it, Neil slithers away to part the tourists from their money, while I head to the toilets to freshen up and piss.

When I come out, I find Neil squatted on the concourse floor with three other people, two men and a girl, a truly mismatched bunch if ever there was one. Neil, of course, stands out like the proverbial turd in a swimming pool, often similarly unwelcome and smelly. Even though he already has some, he is poncing cigarettes. Quite how the other three came to be sitting together, however, is something of a mystery.

One of the two men looks vaguely hippieish, but only insomuch as he has long hair, tied back in a ponytail. He's tough-looking, sinewy, with piercing eyes. He rests against a worn-out rucksack the colour of dead daffodils, rolling himself a cigarette. He pretends not to be listening to

Neil's conversation with the other man, but clearly he is scrutinising my green-haired companion, watching him like a hawk.

The other man has the same sturdy build, but doesn't carry himself with the same confidence. He wears oddly-matched clothes, wrong together, like they were chosen by different people who'd never met him. His nails are bitten to the quick, a lock of dark, greasy hair constantly falling over his large-featured face. He looks nervous, twitchy, perhaps understandably wary that Neil will rob him.

The girl leans forward to introduce herself, shaking my hand in a manner that seems overly formal for the floor of a train station. Her name is Caroline. She's sixteen. Trying to get expelled from some fancy private school to upset Daddy. Overly confident for no good reason other than coming from a wealthy family. Instantly annoying. Wearing white knickers. She doesn't tell me any of this – aside from her name – but she reads like an open book. And I can see her knickers. Presumably she knows this, because she's wearing a long, flowing skirt and yet sitting in such a way as to show them off.

She fires irritating questions at me: What's my real name? How do I spike my hair? Where do I live? Do I have any brothers or sisters? None of your fucking business. She sounds like her mouth is full of marbles, pronounces 'cheers' as 'chairs'. I give her monosyllabic answers, wishing she'd fuck off. Or that we would. But still she blathers on, frightfully excited.

The bloke with the bitten nails, it soon becomes clear, is not quite right in the head. Possibly an outpatient at a local hospital. Possibly an escaped patient. He seems more unbalanced than dangerous, but given my lack of medical expertise that's just conjecture, based largely on the fact that he hasn't stabbed Neil yet.

When I was a child, we lived within walking distance of a place called Weston Manor, an old, Gothic-looking lunatic asylum that has since been turned into a hotel. It was a scary place to walk past, more so during the long winters when it was dark by mid-afternoon and you'd bump into inmates lurking outside the perimeter. You'd see them wandering around town sometimes, too, always looking rather lost. One in particular would buy bags of the same product every day, crisps, sugar, tampons, always a whole bagful of the stuff. Fuck knows where he got the money.

I spent a few afternoons peeking through the fence watching them play rounders, which, at the time, was hilarious. On the rare occasions one of them would actually hit the ball, they'd run off in the wrong direction or not run at all, generally not understanding the rules. Sometimes they'd run off with the bat. Looking back, it was more sad than funny, the inability to play even the simplest games, but I didn't know any better. Besides, they looked like they were enjoying themselves.

The bloke with the bitten nails is like them, probably harmless but ill-fitting in the world like his clothes are ill-fitting on him. The tough-looking hippie is just passing through, but given Caroline's total lack of self-awareness or street smarts he's keeping a gentle eye on her, just to make sure she's safe. He has the look of a traveller and I want to ask him where he's going, where he's been, but Caroline is still gabbing on about nothing. I like the hippie, feel that he's a good person, but I don't think he likes us. Actually, I don't think he has an opinion about me one way or the other, but he definitely doesn't like Neil.

"…and I thought to myself, I just absolutely have to be here today," Caroline drones on and I catch the end of the sentence.

"Why?" I grunt.

"For the wedding, of course!"

"What wedding?"

"The *royal* wedding!" Caroline gasps. "Prince Charles and Lady Diana! Oh my God, how did you not know?"

I didn't know because I didn't care. It was lodged in the back of my mind somewhere that a couple of people I had no interest in were getting hitched at the taxpayers' expense, but somehow the date had managed to escape me. And why wouldn't it? I don't socialize with anyone who'd be remotely interested in such things. Don't socialize with anyone much. But if I did, they wouldn't be interested. The country's going to shit, riots all over the place, and we're supposed to give a crap about some fairy-tale wedding. At least it explains all the flag waving. Apparently I am in the minority.

"Is it a public holiday or something?"

Caroline nods, inhaling on her cigarette, possibly trying to be sexy. She is not remotely sexy. It's not so much that her mouth is too big, both literally and figuratively, nor that her upturned nose is rather pointy. She's actually quite pretty; it's her personality that's ugly, the way she fills the air around herself with her own self-importance.

She's definitely flirting, there's no doubt now. She knows I can see her knickers, knows that I keep glancing at the snowy white, deodorized V, with its neat little crease down the middle. She blabbers on, fluttering her eyelids too much like she's got grit in her eyes, shifting position now and then to afford me another flash of cotton. Worse still, she probably thinks she's being a bad girl, flirting with danger. I am not dangerous, but I know plenty who are. Neil might steal her purse given half a chance, but Razor would follow her home and steal mummy's purse, too. And he's one of the nicer characters.

Sometimes it doesn't even have to do with being intentionally bad; Blue would give her some terrible drug as an act of kindness and then be confused as to why she couldn't handle it, panic and run away when she slipped into a coma. If you know Blue, you know to be extremely wary of any pills he might offer. But she doesn't know Blue, doesn't know anyone outside her circle of friends at the fucking pony club.

Perhaps I'm being unkind. It's not as if I really know her. The alcohol has long worn off and I'm running on fumes, weak like I'll crumble to dust if anyone knocked into me. I leave the four of them talking and head to the toilets to wash myself again in cold water, the dispenser spitting out globs of sticky orange soap. I still feel dirty.

When I get back, the party seems to be coming to a close at last. Daylight is upon us and the hippie has a train to catch. I hover uncomfortably, waiting for them to stand, feeling like I'm looming. They take too long so I sit down, just as they're all standing. The farewells take too long, I just want to go. Anywhere but here. Caroline insists on hugging everyone.

As we are about to leave, she looks at me, suddenly serious. "Can I kiss you?" she asks.

"Uh, yeah, I suppose so." I want to say no.

She leans forward and kisses me on the cheek. Somehow I expected tongues. I feel stupid, used. I should have said no. Now she will brag to her stuck-up friends at the pony club about how she kissed a punk rocker in Victoria station on royal wedding day. The frog who stayed a frog.

I turn to walk away, only to have my path blocked by the nutter with the chewed nails. We do that little dance, both stepping in each other's way, then Neil and I head for the exit, out into the bright morning sunshine. The nutter follows. It takes only moments to lose him in the crowds.

CHAPTER THIRTEEN

IT'S ROUGHLY A mile and a half from Victoria station to Trafalgar Square, but, strangely, I remember nothing at all of the walk. I say strangely, because the route would have taken us either along Victoria Street, past the Houses of Parliament and up Whitehall, or perhaps past Buckingham Palace and along The Mall. Not only would it have been my first time seeing some of those iconic buildings, but there were literally millions of tourists in London for the royal wedding, thousands of them camped outside Buckingham Palace, including later Prime Minister and alleged pig fucker David Cameron. You'd think there would be some memory of it, some flicker of recollection, but, no, it's as if we were suddenly beamed to Trafalgar Square from the deck of the Starship Enterprise.

It would have been early in the morning when we left the station, maybe seven or so, but my first clear memory that day is of sitting by the fountains, around midday, drinking cider. The wedding was already underway at St Paul's Cathedral and although Trafalgar Square was busy, it wasn't particularly crowded. Two million people lined the route of the procession, Fleet Street, maybe Embankment, I don't know. According to Google it passed right by Trafalgar Square on the way to the cathedral, but somehow I missed it and those hours are lost to me. I vaguely remember buying the cider, inadvertently acting as a decoy while Neil stole another bottle, but the wedding procession, the glass carriage, the mad parade... No. That'll be us, sitting by the fountains, getting pissed. To this day I think we made the right choice.

At some point, however, curiosity must have got the better of us, because Neil and I decided to go for a wander down Whitehall, towards whatever might be going on down there. The crowds are thick here, several rows deep, pressed up against metal barriers, happy, smiling, flag-waving sheep, all straining to catch a glimpse of fuck knows what. Grinning parasites. A fairy-tale wedding that ultimately ended in disaster. Whatever love is…

Even then, the wedding seemed to be nothing more than a political gesture, another decoy, with rather more at stake than a bottle of cider. Massive unemployment figures and nationwide rioting, but look over here at the shiny things. And we look. Seven hundred million viewers worldwide.

What difference would a couple more make?

We get no more than about two hundred yards, Neil and I, before quickly discovering that some guests are rather less welcome than others.

The ruthless efficiency with which we are snatched from the street is terrifying. One minute we're ambling peacefully through the crowds, the next we are grabbed by the arms and hauled through a large, wooden door. From the street, you'd probably think it was the entrance to a building, if you noticed it at all. But on the other side is a quiet alleyway, where our four assailants identify themselves as plain-clothes police officers.

The alleyway is cool in contrast to the heat of the streets, empty but for a few rubbish bins, silent, no sound from the crowds outside. No one would even suspect we are here. It all happened so fast that no one even noticed, so fast that there is no time to think. Before we know what's going on we're pinned to the wall. One of the cops has his hand around my throat, slowly cutting off my ability to breathe as he makes it abundantly clear that our invitations to these royal celebrations were not lost in the post. They ask us no questions, no names or dates of birth. The message is clear and simple; go away and don't come back.

"You and your fucking boyfriend are going to leave here quickly and quietly," the cop snarls, his face so close to mine that he could kiss me. A small irony. "Understand?"

I try to nod, but merely end up blinking my acknowledgement of this one-sided but increasingly attractive proposition.

"Under-fucking-stand?" he bangs the back of my head against the wall as if knocking the message in.

"Yes," I squeak.

"Good. Now fuck off and don't come back!"

We are bundled back into the heat and sunshine, dazzled and disorientated by the light, Neil collecting a stinging punch to the ear on the way out. We don't look back. The encounter lasts no more than a few minutes but in many ways lasts a lifetime. I get a slap around the face, a dig in the ribs, but it's not as if we're beaten up. The bruises fade, but the loss of innocence never leaves me, the loss of trust.

When I was fifteen years old I ran away from home. Such was policing in the small town that the local policeman, I'm told, spent his day off looking for me, worried that I might be in trouble. He knew all the punks by name and knew our parents' names. At worst we might get a telling-off for misbehaving. Two weeks later, having lived largely on a diet of wild blackberries, I gave myself up, calling another local cop whose number I found in the phone book. It was his day off, too, so he was a bit grumpy, not really wanting to deal with the paperwork, but he did his job. Of course, I'd heard about police brutality, the savage beating of Clarence Baker by the SPG, the deaths of Liddle Towers and Blair Peach, but somehow that was another world. I watched the *Sweeney*, but lived in *Dixon Of Dock Green*. If you want to know the time, ask a policeman. Now that had all changed. I still don't hold with the reasoning that all coppers are bastards. But some are complete cunts.

We head quickly back to Trafalgar Square and take no further interest in the royal celebrations. On a balcony at Buckingham Palace, Prince Charles is reluctantly kissing his new bride. So much for fairy tales.

There are maybe a dozen punks in the square, relieving the tourists of their spare change and posing for photographs. I quickly learn that the tourists, particularly the Americans, are happy to pay for pictures, and so begins a lucrative career in modelling. Within a few hours I've made almost as much as I would for a full week working in the factory. I also learn that certain tourists are rather sneaky and will stand nearby, ostensibly taking pictures of the fountains but actually taking pictures of punks. They are generally told to fuck off.

There is a punk girl in the square who deals with such tourists in a particularly aggressive fashion, shooing them away like pigeons, occasionally chasing after them to demand her 'modelling fee'. Sporting a Mohican haircut with two long spikes on either side, and heavy eye make-up, she wears a tartan miniskirt, fishnet stockings, motorcycle boots, and a T-shirt with 'Fuck The Mods' printed on the front, her ensemble completed by chains, safety pins and razorblades. She looks fierce but has a pretty smile when she allows it onto her face. She's French and her name is Corrine.

We spend the next few hours posing for pictures together, pretending to be a couple because the tourists are inclined to hand over more money. Every now and then Corrine dashes after the sneaky ones, flapping her arms about, telling them to "ferk off!" Some time during the afternoon we stop pretending. Her kisses taste of bubblegum.

More punks drift into the square, and there are rumours that somewhere in London Crass will be playing an anti-royalist gig from the back of a truck, perhaps in Trafalgar Square, no one seems to know exactly. It's entirely in keeping with the band's subversive nature and there's a buzz of excitement about the idea, but it seems a little late in the day for such a protest. The wedding was over long ago. And given the heavy-handed treatment that Neil and I received earlier just for wanting to *look* at the royal spectacle, it's probably a good thing the gig never happened.

Among the new arrivals is another French girl, a friend of Corrine's, who goes by the name of Emmanuelle, presumably not because of the 1974 mainstream porn movie of the same name. She is stunningly pretty, petite, with short-cropped, black hair and porcelain skin, no make up, just natural beauty. She wears black combat trousers, black boots and a black T-shirt. I get the sense, immediately, that she has been damaged in some way, perhaps abused as a child. She has an air of fragility about her, but in the same way that broken glass is fragile. Maybe once she was a victim, but now she will cut you if you mess with her. On her left arm is a small tattoo: Fuck law and order.

Completely failing to read any of these signs, Neil wanders over and starts trying to chat her up.

"Gis a fag, yeah?" he suggests.

She doesn't stab him.

I'm surprised to learn that Emmanuelle works as a waitress in a swanky restaurant; clearly she doesn't like humans. She covers her tattoo for work, but it's hard to imagine her treating the customers with anything other than the utmost contempt, harder still to imagine her smiling at them. It's also a surprise to find out that Corrine has a job as a bartender. She's cheerful enough, friendly when she's not chasing sneaky tourists away, but her appearance is full-on and can't be toned down even if she wanted to. She has work tonight and invites me along for some free drinks. Apparently, there's a band playing, but she can't remember the name.

And so the day passes, hanging out, drinking cider and having our pictures taken. Neil hasn't really got the hang of the whole modelling thing and sticks largely to demanding spare change, but no one seems to mind too much. It's a beautiful lazy day and life is good. Corrine says we can stay at the squat in Vauxhall that she shares with Emmanuelle, and as evening draws near we head for the tube station. Four stops south on the Northern line, one stop north on the Victoria line, a short walk from the tube station.

Coronation Buildings is – or was – a cluster of four ugly tower blocks built around 1905, adjacent to the railway line on South Lambeth Road. It was in a terrible state of disrepair and most of the flats that hadn't been taken over by squatters were abandoned. There were no lights on the ground floor and no lifts. Corrine lived on the forth or fifth floor.

Keen to refresh my memory, I searched on Google and found an old black and white photograph of the place. Which led, of course, to more poking. Maybe I'd find some more pictures or a little history of the buildings, something more than when they were built and the fact that they were demolished to make way for office blocks. What I find instead is utterly horrifying.

Around the time I would have been staying there, certainly around the time that Corrine was living there, one of the flats was under surveillance as part of a three-month operation to uncover a paedophile ring that had connections to the highest levels of government. Video footage from a camera set up inside the flat showed young boys being abused, but when police tried to make arrests they were warned away, their livelihoods and families threatened. One of those accused was Sir Cyril Smith MP, a truly loathsome human being, 420 pounds of blubber, like Jabba the Hutt with a hard-on for children. He was never convicted, but since his death in 2010 it has been reported that there were no less than 144 allegations made against him, dating back to the '60s, some from children as young as eight years old. He was the literal elephant in the room, preying on kids who were supposed to be in care. Attempts to prosecute him were always blocked. Evidence was destroyed. It makes for difficult reading, to say the least. More so because so many people knew about it and did nothing to stop it.

Perhaps, at the time, I was no more than a few floors away from the flat in question, completely unaware of the horror. Perhaps I was lucky not to have found myself amidst that horror. Either way, I'm glad they've knocked the fucking place down.

CHAPTER FOURTEEN

CORRINE'S SQUAT IS Sparsely furnished, a mattress, a wooden chair, a cupboard for clothes, no carpet, bare wooden floors. It's a two bedroom flat with the living room used as an extra bedroom, because one of the bedrooms has no floorboards. There's a small kitchen and bathroom. The paint is peeling from the walls, but it has electricity and running water, hot and cold. Emmanuelle and Neil have gone elsewhere, so we have the place to ourselves. Corrine gets ready for work, a clean T-shirt and a fresh coat of make-up, while I gaze out of the filthy window, entranced by the beautiful, filthy city below.

It's strange now to reminisce about places that would later become so familiar, so mundane, but I could have stared out of that window all night, enchanted and lost in the magic of London. Instead, when Corrine's ready, we head back to the tube station and bunk the train to Covent Garden. The place is a tourist trap, increasingly littered with homogeneous crap like The Body Shop, Starbucks and Urban Decay, but there are always cool little shops like custom jewellers The Crazy Pig, and there's always some kind of street theatre going on, artists, buskers and acrobats. Unfortunately the trend is not for the better. The Crazy Pig's still there, but so, too, is Gap.

The Rock Garden, where Corrine worked, is now the world's largest Apple store, because that's just what the place needed instead of a thriving rock venue and restaurant. It sat on the corner of James Street, a fancy-looking restaurant with al fresco dining by the piazza – or at least fancy-looking to a seventeen-year-old punk – and a door to the left leading down a narrow staircase to the small club.

We arrive before the club is open and Corrine pours me a lager before setting up whatever needs doing for her shift. Perched on a bar stool, I'm on my second drink before anyone shows up, but it gets crowded fairly fast, mostly rowdy Australian tourists as far as I can tell. I stay at my spot by the bar and don't really talk to anyone. Corrine's busy serving drinks, but she refills my glass whenever it's empty. Pretty soon the place is packed.

I don't remember an opening band. What I remember, quite vividly, is the appearance of some escaped lunatics onstage, and a sudden change in the audience from boisterous to downright aggressive, all heaving and shoving, almost but never quite fighting. The lunatics seemed to thrive on this aggression, empowered by it, all the more menacing for their revelling in this barely suppressed violence. The singer was stick-thin, shirtless, and clearly deranged, howling and barking, wild-eyed beneath a bird's nest of black hair. His name was Nick Cave and the band was called The Birthday Party.

Although I was lucky enough to see the band several times after that night, it was that first show that is forever embedded in my mind. Not just songs like *King Ink*, *Nick The Stripper* and *Release The Bats*, all of them delivered with a manic intensity, all of them classics, but the mesmerizing stage presence, the unrestrained madness. The sheer fucking *genius!*

I remember being particularly impressed by the bass player Tracy Pew, a bulldozer of a man in leather trousers, mesh T-shirt and cowboy hat; a freak who could kick your ass if you dared to call him such. Probably had to be with a name like Tracy. I liked that. Obviously, they were a bass-heavy band, a crawling psychobilly blues, but there was something special about him, an outlaw spirit. I was saddened but not surprised to learn that he was just 28 years old when he died.

But, Christ, they were a good band while they lasted. Just thinking about it now makes me want to go out and get all crazy, but, alas, it's not every day that you stumble across the perfect moment in the eye of the storm. More likely I'd just wake up with a shitty hangover and not get any writing done.

When it's over I wait for Corrine to finish her shift, sliding me another drink that I don't really need before she closes up the bar. Thankfully, someone else has to clean up the rest of the mess, the spilt beer and broken glasses. Then we head out into Covent Garden, a different place by night, bathed in the warm glow of street lights, alive with night people heading home or to some place where the bars are still open.

We get the last tube to Vauxhall, another different place by night, fast moving cars and long, mean shadows. There's an air of menace about these empty streets, no warmth about these street lights. Here they pick us out as targets and we walk quickly. Corrine's place is not far, but no more welcoming until we've climbed the many stairs and locked the door behind us. Emmanuelle's bedroom door is closed and there's no sound to suggest that she's home, so we are alone together. Even though we've kissed today and walked hand in hand, I'm glad when Corrine makes the first move.

I'm woken too early by the morning sun coming in through the curtainless window, warm beams of light fighting their way past the dirt and inching slowly across the floor towards the bed. I try to get back to sleep, but my mind seems to think that three hours sleep in as many days is all I need. The room smells of sex and sweat. Outside, the city is coming alive. The rat race has begun. I wait for Corrine to wake up so we can make the room more smelly.

We're naked on the bed, smoking post-coital cigarettes, when Emmanuelle's door opens.

"Alight, yeah?"

"Fuck's sake, Neil!" I hastily pull the sheet up to cover us.

"What?"

"You could have knocked."

"Gis a fag, yeah?"

I pass him a cigarette, then another when I realise that he's not alone. As unlikely as it might be that he's spent the night with Emmanuelle without getting stabbed, it's even less likely that he's been sitting in her room alone. I'm rather hoping that they were already here when we got in last night and didn't sneak past us while we were asleep, not least because Neil might have felt inclined to go through my pockets. Either way they'll have heard us fucking, which is not really something I want to think about.

Neil, I notice, is still fully dressed. Indeed, still wearing the same clothes he was in when I met him.

Eventually we get out of bed, and after Corrine has refreshed her warpaint, we head out into the world, making our way, once more, to Trafalgar Square. Already there are half a dozen or so punks lurking about, parting the tourists from their cash, and we join them for a few hours before Corrine suggests going to find some food. A novel idea given that I haven't eaten anything more substantial than a bag of crisps in about four days.

We walk north from Trafalgar Square, past the National Portrait Gallery and up Charing Cross Road, before making a left onto a narrow side street, where we find a fish and chip shop. We get a bag of chips each and eat them outside on the pavement, then decide to find an off-licence so we can get some booze. Then, suitably furnished with bottles of warm cider, we make our way along Shaftesbury Avenue, turning right on Wardour Street where we find a small park.

I say 'find', but in fact it's been there since 1686, overlooked by the imposing tower of St Anne's Church, for which it served as a burial ground until 1853, when burials were stopped by an act of parliament. Officially opened as a public garden in 1892, it's estimated that over 100,000 burials took place here, and the site still contains several memorials and gravestones. Fuck knows where they put so many bodies given the limited space, but it's a nice retreat from the hustle of Soho, and not an unpleasant place to get drunk. Assuming, of course, that such things are still permitted. Once there were low, black iron railings across the entrance of the park, but now there is a stainless steel security fence, known as The Wall of Light because it employs fibre optic lighting that lights up at night with different colours. According to the official website, the fence was installed because 'the churchyard became a meeting place for drug addicts and dealers', which is rather like finally noticing that the sea is full of fish, but I rather hope you're still allowed to get pissed there on a hot summer afternoon.

We're about halfway across the park, striding towards a patch of sunshine on the grass, when I catch sight of Neil, deep in conversation with a stubby, ginger-haired wino with a bright red face. We ignore him, hoping he hasn't spotted us, but no such luck.

"Oi!" he bellows out across the peace, silencing birdsong from a nearby tree. "Over 'ere!"

We ignore him some more and sit ourselves down, but he wafts over like bad smell, with the ginger wino in tow. He momentarily blocks out the sun, bringing goosebumps to my arms, then dumps himself on the grass beside us.

"Gis a fag."

"None left," I lie.

Unabashed, Neil takes a pack from his pocket and lights one, failing to offer them around. The wino, a haggard-looking, middle-aged man with a squashed nose and a face like a burglar's dog, plonks down with him, half falling, half sitting, gleefully eyeing my unopened cider. He manages to focus long enough to give me a hopeful, toothless grin, but there's no way he's getting his rotten mouth anywhere near the bottle. Neither of them seem to comprehend that they're not welcome.

Come to think of it, Westminster council were probably on to something with their rather ugly fence. Neil and Ginger eventually take the hint and leave us alone, but for every tourist or office worker enjoying a few hours in the sunshine there are two or three winos and junkies to hassle them. Peace returns to our little patch of grass, but not for long.

The first to bother us is a wiry-looking skinhead with bad facial tattoos, Made In London across his throat.

"Lensafag," he slurs, off his face on a downer or some sort, possibly Tuinal.

"What?"

"Lensafag."

"Lend you a fag?"

"Yeah," he sneers, apparently unaware of the words 'please' and 'thank you'.

I consider, for a moment, asking when he intends to pay back this loan, but I just want him to go away. I give him a cigarette and he doesn't go away.

"Lens fifty pee."

"Got no money."

"Lens a swig of your cider."

"No."

"Oh, g'on."

"No."

Corrine tells him to fuck off.

Unfortunately, the next chancer – a Scottish lunatic with pupils the size of pinheads – is not so easily deterred. He has a bottle scar around his left eye, a piece missing out of his nose, and an accent so thick you could plaster a wall with it. He keeps calling me Ken and it takes a while to figure out that this is Scottish for 'understand'. It takes a while longer, mentally rearranging the vowels, to figure out that he's trying to sell us drugs. He becomes aggressive when I tell him I've got no money.

"Ah ken yuv goat money," he growls. "'Mon, man."

"No, really, I'm fucking broke, mate."

He is not my mate by any stretch of the imagination. I subtly change the grip on my cider bottle in case I have to hit him with it.

"Supply 'n' deman' ken?" he persists, apparently failing to comprehend that there is no demand. "'Mon, man, wur hud a deal."

We most certainly did not have a deal. Even if I wanted drugs I wouldn't be wanting whatever the fuck he's taken. He's not what you'd call a good advertisement for his wares, worse still when he digs into his pocket and presents us with a handful of yellow mush and dirt that may once have been half a dozen pills. I'm guessing Valium, but they could be anything. Since he won't go away, the only thing we can do is make our excuses and leave. So much for a quiet afternoon in the park. I kind of hope that new fence is electrified.

CHAPTER FIFTEEN

ON ANY GIVEN day, should you decide that sanity is overrated and that what you really need is to be struggling through endless crowds of gormless shoppers and tourists, you should pay a visit to Oxford Street. It really is quite horrible, a vile cacophony of traffic, belching fumes, people not looking where the fuck they're going, dodgy street vendors and… Well, just don't go there. As I write, the street is closed off due to a stabbing.

Should you decide to ignore this sound advice, however, you will inevitably encounter a gaggle of orange-clad Hare Krishnas weaving and bobbing their way through the crowds, banging drums, ringing bells, and generally making an unnecessary racket. Which they always appear to be unduly happy about. Although, to be fair, theirs are probably the only smiling faces you'll see on Oxford Street.

Their headquarters are on Soho Street, a temple and restaurant just north of Soho Square, and it's here that Corrine and I find ourselves as we search for another quiet place to drink. We were actually heading for the square, another small oasis of calm in central London, but as we round the corner from Oxford Street our path is blocked by a green-haired idiot in a swastika T-shirt. Clutching a half bottle of rum, he is loudly arguing with a couple of Hare Krishnas about the necessity to eat meat, vigorously maintaining that those who abstain from bacon sandwiches are "cunts".

"Alright, Neil, gis a swig," I break him off mid-rant, sensing relief on the faces of the Krishnas.

I can't help noticing that one of them has SKINS tattooed on his neck, so while Neil and Corrine set about fleecing passing tourists, I get chatting to him out of curiosity. I wouldn't claim to know a great deal about their faith, but, haircuts aside, there can't be many similarities between skinheads and Krishnas. Unfortunately, I learn very little.

Krishna Skin, it transpires, is a recent convert, and while he's happy to talk, he doesn't really say much. Just a bunch of spiritual psychobabble that doesn't make a lot of sense. From what I can gather, Krishna is something to do with the god Vishnu, but also a god in his own right. The god of compassion, tenderness and love, to be precise. Which is an improvement on the beardy bastard who's known for smiting people, and certainly an improvement for Krishna Skin, but still doesn't offer any real answers. While the streets are undoubtedly a little safer thanks to his conversion, it would appear that he's just swapped one cult for another, boots and braces for an orange robe.

At this point, Neil returns and sticks his nose into the conversation, feigning interest and managing to invite us along for a free vegetarian meal tomorrow on the condition that we join the Krishnas in prayer or something. We leave before they have a chance to change their minds, hopping the tube from Tottenham Court Road back to Vauxhall. Neil wasn't invited, but he comes along anyway. It's kind of a habit.

The trouble with having your bedroom in the living room, as I discover when we get back to Corrine's place, is that, perhaps not surprisingly, people tend to use it as a living room. Also not surprisingly, Corrine is not too happy about having half a dozen punks in her room when she just wants to chill out before getting ready for work. There follows a heated argument in French, the gist of it being, as far as I can gather, that Emmanuelle has guests and Corrine wants them all to fuck off. It doesn't take a strong grasp of the language to work this out, the shouting and slamming doors are a clue. No one else seems to notice.

I recognise a couple of the faces but wouldn't be able to put names to them. It's not as if anyone bothers with introductions. Except Neil, of course, who immediately latches onto a sharply pretty blonde girl, possibly an ex-skinhead, with one of those Chelsea haircuts. He sits beside her on the bed, all smiles.

"Gis a fag, yeah?"

"Fack off and buy yer own."

Undeterred, Neil tries his luck with the others and gets much the same response. Tough crowd. I like them. It's not as if he hasn't got cigarettes, he's just completely shameless and incapable of turning off 'ponce mode'.

Half an hour later Corrine and Emmanuelle are still arguing, and still no one else seems to have noticed or seems to feel remotely uncomfortable about being the cause of it. Since Corrine is technically sort of my girlfriend, I feel obliged to take the initiative and at least get me and Neil out of there in the hope that the others will follow. Which they don't.

There's a band called the Au Pairs playing an Anti-Nazi League benefit at Brixton Town Hall, kind of an indie-punk thing, and while I'm only familiar with one of their songs, the sublimely brilliant *It's Obvious,* it turns out to be an inspired choice. The internet tells me now that the opening bands were the Pinkies and the Outskirts, of whom I remember nothing at all, and although the gig is decent enough, pleasantly mellow and full of student types sporting Rock Against Racism badges, it's Brixton itself that conjures the most vivid memories. A wonderful place that seems, against all odds, to be fighting off the worst of gentrification.

In the years to come I would get the chance to explore these vibrant streets, from dodgy back alleys with dodgier cab ranks and the hustle of drug dealers, to the mansions of the wealthy. Including one that was owned by a lord, who regularly invited the Hells Angels over to party. Perhaps a story for another time. Let's just say that good times were had. Brixton also has some of the capital's best clubs and music venues.

But the streets were eerily and uncharacteristically quiet that night of my first visit in 1981. Maybe we loitered around the venue long enough for the audience to disperse, but there was hardly anyone around when we came out. No revellers heading to and from clubs. No music. No one waiting for night buses. Very little passing traffic. Just Neil and I walking the streets.

Just a few months earlier, between April 10th and 12th, there was fierce rioting here with nearly 300 police injured and hundreds of cars and buildings torched, as an estimated 5,000 people protested police harassment in the only way they knew how. A couple of months later, on the 10th of July, it all kicked off again, the riots spreading like wildfire to Battersea,

Streatham, Dalston, Walthamstow, Southall, Birmingham, Southampton, Luton, Leicester, Manchester, Leeds, and many other places too numerous to mention. It seemed like the whole country was in flames.

As far as Brixton is concerned it began... Well, it began decades earlier, when the police apparently had an appalling practice that they called 'Nigger Hunting', letting their dogs loose to chase black people. Race relations were, to put it mildly, strained. By 1981 tensions had reached boiling point with the introduction of Operation Swamp 81 – named for a statement by then Prime Minister Thatcher about the area being "swamped with immigrants" – which allowed police to stop and search people under some obscure vagrancy act dating back to 1824. Within five days nearly 1,000 people had been stopped and 82 arrests made, often young black men fitted up for crimes they hadn't committed. As you'd imagine the 'sus' law, as it became known, was not popular. Especially since the police involved were either plain-clothed or members of the notoriously violent Special Patrol Group, whose unauthorised arsenal of weapons included baseball bats, crowbars and sledgehammers. Tired of being pushed, Brixton pushed back, and the rest of the country followed.

No doubt, there's more to it than that, massive unemployment, poor housing, and by all accounts some confusion, on that first night in April, about the stabbing of a young black man. But either way, the streets exploded, and the sus law was repealed by August of '81.

So, the streets were empty that night, just a couple of weeks after the last disturbances. I don't recall seeing any signs of violence, no fire-damaged property or gutted cars, no broken glass. Instead, I remember that on the walk back to Vauxhall Neil and I passed the police station on Brixton Road and found it guarded by police, just in case anyone tried to burn it down. They watched us as we passed, perhaps no more than a few minutes that seem forever frozen in time. Us looking at them. Them looking at us. A curious spell had been cast that night. A spell that is broken not half an hour later when we could really have done with seeing some cops.

We're walking back to Vauxhall, peaceful, just chatting and laughing. Mostly at the expense of a girl I met at the gig who wouldn't leave me alone. Her name was Jemma and she started talking to me at the bar, then wouldn't stop. A nice girl, I'm sure, but painfully sincere as she babbled on about left-wing causes, racism, feminism, and lots of other words ending in ism. Not that I disagreed, I just didn't see how two white kids at an Anti-Nazi League gig jawing on about equal rights was going to change the world. We were already at the gig, already on the same side, and unless we were planning to ambush a National Front march, which we were not, it was all just so much hot air. To make matters worse, she had a notice-able speech impediment, so when she started going on about her thesis I giggled like a small child because it sounded like faeces.

But still she wouldn't go away.

That is until Neil showed up, eating, in the most disgusting fashion, a sandwich he had found on the floor, and clutching a cracked plastic beer glass full of warm piss. He gave her an equally warm smile, proudly displaying a mouthful of half-chewed food. Which would have been the optimum time for her to go away. But she didn't.

"Alright, yeah?" He took a swig. "You want some?"

"Oh, thank you, yes," said the girl. The stupid, stupid girl.

The night was hot and she took a generous gulp. A look of confusion and then horror crossed her face. And *then* she left, dashing from the table towards the toilets, presumably to throw up.

"Wos the matter wiv 'er?" Neil grunted.

"Problem with her poo," I said. "She's been going on about it all night."

So, we're walking along, quietly drunk, Neil swigging on a half empty bottle of cider that he found in a rubbish bin, to wash down the chicken wings he found in the same bin. There is something sticky smeared on the bottle that has attracted dirt. Neil hasn't bothered to wipe it off. Then, suddenly, a car goes speeding past in the opposite direction and someone yells out of the window.

"Wankers!"

"Fuck off!" Neil yells back, offering a two-digit salute.

Brake lights. Fuck.

I keep walking, quickening my pace, hoping they're just trying to scare us. But no, the car is stopping, the passenger door already open. There are four of them in the car – pubby-looking thugs – but thankfully it's a two-door hatchback so they can't all get out at once. We're also separated by four lanes, which is a decent head start, but unfortunately Neil is rather more drunk – or rather more stupid – than I suspected, and decides to stand his ground.

Traffic builds up out of nowhere, fast moving cars preventing them from crossing the road, but three of the four thugs are out of their vehicle, striding purposefully in our direction. The driver is still behind the wheel, but only because he can't park where he's stopped. Doubtless he'd have done a U-turn if it wasn't for the centre divide. We need to move. Now!

"Neil, fuck's sake!"

But Neil is having none of it.

"Yeah? You want some, you wankers?" he yells.

Obviously they want some. Any idiot can see that. It wouldn't take a genius to also work out that we'll be on the wrong side of a kicking if they manage to catch us. But Neil, apparently, is not a genius. A lull in the traffic allows two of the three thugs to reach the centre divide upon which they dart back and forth, waiting for another gap. At this point, the 'genius' lobs his cider bottle at them, glass smashing all over the road as it falls short of its target. And with all the loyalty of a beloved family dog... I run away!

CHAPTER SIXTEEN

THE ADRENALINE RUSH that comes with narrowly escaping a serious beating is unlike any other. I'd imagine that skydiving is similar. Except that with skydiving you can be reasonably certain, unless you're a complete imbecile and have jumped out of a plane without a parachute, that said parachute will deploy when you pull the ripcord, so you won't get your head smashed in. Running away from nutters offers no such guarantees. Only the guarantee of a smashed in head if you get it wrong.

Fortunately, Neil comes to his senses and takes to his heels right behind me. Unfortunately, he takes off like a fucking jackrabbit and quickly overtakes me, which again brings to mind the old adage about outrunning lions. Namely that you don't have to, you just have to outrun whoever you're with. Neil isn't hanging about! And neither are the nutters, two of them on our side of the road now, another running parallel on the other side.

There's a junction at the end of the road and Neil vaults the railings, sprinting across a couple of lanes and over more railings. I'm not far behind and once again the traffic is our ally, allowing me to leg it across, then building up, fast moving, to stop our pursuers. A sudden smash on the opposite pavement has two of them dancing like their boots are on fire. Neil has found a couple of crates of empty milk bottles and is lobbing them with varying degrees of accuracy across the road. I join him, my first shot falling short and bouncing off the roof of a passing car. The car swerves and speeds away wanting no part of this madness.

But both time and bottles are running out. Across the road, the third nutter is over the railings, looking for gaps in the traffic. He's armed with a length of scaffolding pole. Christ knows where he got it, but it doesn't bode well for when the lights change. In a manner that looks all too sober, he bashes the weapon against the railings as he paces back and forth.

"Come on, you cunts! Let's fucking 'ave it!"

We decline his offer and run. I don't know where we're running, but away will do for now. Anywhere but here. Through a short tunnel, a railway arch, our footsteps echoing into the night. I catch up with Neil, almost tripping over his heels, not sure why he seems to have slowed down except that he might be out of breath. Neck and neck like we're sprinting for the finish line in some bizarre sporting event. The hundred metre dash for the resolutely unfit. Fifteen hundred metre relay for the terminally afraid. My heart is beating like the start of *New Rose*. Cars flash past, shocked white faces peering out. My kingdom for a police car.

And then, just as suddenly as it began, the chase is over. I have no idea why. Maybe the nutters just gave up. Maybe they found some other poor sods to pick on. All I know is that they're gone. Ours not to reason why.

We proceed with caution, sticking to the shadows like feral cats.

Years later, perhaps twenty years or so, I was walking under that same archway on Parry Street, heading to an underground and possibly illegal fetish club, when, suddenly, I had a moment of realization. This was the place. I must have been past it a thousand times as a motorcycle messenger, but it never once dawned on me. And yet here we were following a rubber-clad transvestite who tottered along on high heels with barely a second glance from passers-by. Times change. Sometimes even for the better.

The adrenaline is still pumping, giving us fits of the giggles as we climb the stairs at Coronation Buildings. We knock on the door, all smiles, but the look of thunder on Corrine's face instantly wipes them away. Something's not right here. Are we taking the piss by turning up at one o'clock in the morning? Is she still arguing with Emmanuelle? Is there still a gaggle of unwelcome punks in her room? But no, it's worse than that. We're ushered inside, and there in her bedroom are two very large skinheads.

Immediately, we size each other up, like dogs on the same council estate. We're clearly at a disadvantage if they decide to take us on but somehow invincible, still buzzing after our recent escape from the nutters outside. The skinheads stare at us and we stare back, unflinching, arrogant, too stupid to back down. The weird stand-off seems to last hours but is probably no more than a few seconds, and then Corrine is introducing us like we're long-lost brothers, over-familiar, defusing the situation by throwing in the names of mutual friends to establish common ground. I know none of these names.

The bigger skinhead, Rob, nods almost respectfully but offers no smile, and the stand-off is over, neither side sullied or dishonoured. Cunt that he is, Neil takes the opportunity to make himself scarce and leave us to it.

"I'm goin' t' bed," he mutters, and disappears into Emmanuelle's room.

Corrine, meanwhile, still all fake smiles, leads me into the tiny kitchen on the premise of making tea. Here she whispers at me that the skinheads showed up shortly after she got home from work, looking, they said, for one of the girls that was here earlier. When told that she wasn't here they said they'd wait. And now they won't go away. Clearly rattled, Corrine has been alone with them ever since. She has no idea who they are. We make them tea.

And so begins one of the longest nights of my life, as tedious as it is terrifying.

Rob is a lump in ever possible way. Thicker than a sack of cement, he's what people refer to as 'big boned'. Hands the size of frying pans. Knuckles like a sackful of bricks. He is Dim from A Clockwork Orange. A mindless grinning bulldog.

But it's Joe who really frightens me, a wiry-looking bastard with shark-cold eyes and about as much sense of logic as a cement mixer. A truly nasty piece of work. He takes great delight in regaling us with tales of the horrific violence he's inflicted on pretty much anyone he's ever come into contact with, and leaves me with absolutely no doubt that he'll do the same to me on a whim. Laugh in the wrong place and he'll cut your face with a razor. Fail to laugh in the right place and he'll smack you in the teeth with an ashtray. It's possible he'll do both just because he's bored, just to liven things up a bit.

Both of them seem to enjoy violence, but while Rob appears to be vaguely rational, albeit with the mental capacity of a box of rocks, Joe is clearly a fucking nutcase. A bad wiring job that's totally wired. I can't tell if he's on drugs, possibly a mixture of Tuinal and speed, but it's doesn't make a lot of difference. Either way, he's a horrible cunt.

"So, this geezer's started, right?" Joe recalls ruefully, shaking his head as if at the memory of a small child dropping its ice cream. "I know he's gonnarav a pop, like, so I've got me 'ands up, defensive, like I don't want none of it. But I've got this bottle offa the bar, spanked 'im inna teef wiv it and 'e goes down like a fuckin' decka cards…"

"Decka cards," repeats Rob, being beyond all shadow of a doubting Thomas, the dimmest of we four. He contributes only slightly more in the way of intelligent conversation than Corrine, who is asleep.

Not that I blame her in the least. Although I can't say I feel the same generosity towards Neil for abandoning me to these fucking psychos. I'm tempted to go and wake him up, but deterred by the fact that he might annoy them. Maybe it's better to let sleeping cunts lie. If it wasn't for Corrine, I'd leave him to fend for himself; tell the two boneheads that I'm going for a walk to find some cigarettes or something and just keep walking. Then again, given our earlier encounter, it might not be any safer out on the streets at this time of night, and there's always the chance that they'd decide to come with me. Fuck that for a game of soldiers. Better to wait until daylight and hope we can get rid of them.

But while it never gets truly dark in London, dawn is a long way off, and still these lunatics have tales to tell, Joe pacing the small room like a caged tiger as he relives yet another battle on the football terraces. This one involves throwing sharpened coins over the fence at rival fans, which is apparently a common practice. Like it's perfectly normal to spend hours on end filing down your spare change and lobbing it at people in the hope of inflicting serious injury upon them. Casual violence, random violence, racist violence, homophobic violence, you name it, these two have done it. The trick is to stop them doing it to me.

I consciously lower my IQ as much as possible without dribbling, pretend to be interested and impressed, and agree with anything they say no matter how appalling. This is no time for questions or debate, no time to be defending minorities. Call me a coward. I know I'm guilty of complicity by not speaking out, but it's not like I can say anything that will change their ways, at least not while they're together. Rob seems like he'll just follow the herd and might be persuaded to change if he were in better company, but Joe is on a fast track to prison. Or back to prison, since he's already done a "shit and shave for ABH", meaning a short sentence for actual bodily harm. A mere eight months for glassing someone.

"Anen there was that time outside the fuckin' Rainbow," Joe prattles on as I struggle to look attentive. "'Member that, Rob? That little Paki bloke…"

"Paki bloke," nods Rob.

And they're off again. Another vile story about ruining someone's life. Christ, will it never end? Why won't they go away? I'm tempted to go to sleep, but fearful of what they'll do if I close my eyes. Doubtless they'd steal what few possessions we have, because even though I'd be powerless to stop them my being conscious somehow acts as a deterrent. But, dear God, please make them shut up. I don't want to hear about any more fights or mates that I've never met, have no interest in, and would cross the whole country to avoid. Instead, I light another cigarette, chain-smoking to stay awake.

At long last there is a faint glow outside, the pink hue of early morning through the filthy window, and slowly, so slowly the dawning of a beautiful new day. It looks like being another scorcher, not a cloud in the sky. Just two large clouds in the room.

Looking all too well-rested, Neil finally emerges from the other room in search of cigarettes. I'm quite glad that they're all gone and take some little joy in the fact that he doesn't ask Joe or Rob for one. Corrine wakes next, blurry-eyed and not at all happy to see them still here. She makes tea and starts dropping hints that they should fuck off. Emmanuelle's not here and neither is the girl they were waiting for, perhaps they'd have better luck elsewhere. But these two wouldn't take a hint if it was tied to a paving slab and dropped on them from the top of a tower block. Subtleties are completely wasted. I'd say they'd outstayed their welcome if they had ever been welcome.

In the end, it's Neil who does the trick. Who is better lacking in subtleties?

"I'm goin' up town to ponce some money," he grunts. "You coming?"

At first I think he's just talking to the skinheads, doing the decent thing and getting them out of here. But, no, of course not. The bastard's talking to me. I desperately need sleep, a bath, some time alone with Corrine, but somehow it's clear that if I go with Neil then the skinheads will go too. If I stay then they'll stay. As much as I hate to admit it, I think they like me. I exchange glances with Corrine, apology in her eyes, resignation in mine. There really is no choice.

"I'm not working tonight," she whispers as we kiss goodbye. "I'll wait in for you."

It's bright when we get outside, already a sticky heat falling over the city. A brand new day, full of exciting possibilities. The most exciting of which is getting rid of two horrible skinheads.

CHAPTER SEVENTEEN

RUSH HOUR. THE train clatters into the station and comes to a halt with a series of terrible screeching noises. Doors open. People hustle forward to get in, then see us and think better of it, moving hurriedly to a different carriage. By the time we get to Victoria the train is packed, standing room only. But no one stands near us. I can't say I blame them. These are straight people, nine-to-five people, mortgage people. They try not to look at us, eyes firmly fixed on the Samaritans advert, rereading the advert for holidays in Greece for all the family. Anything but look at the vile spectacle that despoils their morning commute.

Neil has cracked open a bottle of rum that may have been better shared last night. I have no idea where he got it, but I'm glad when he passes it around, gulping down as much as I can swallow before passing it to Rob. By the time we reach Green Park station it's gone. Finished in one stop. It burns all the way down and doesn't sit well on an empty stomach. I didn't think to ask where we're going, but apparently we have to change trains and I have difficulty standing up, bouncing into commuters as we stagger along the long, busy tunnels to the next train. If not for Joe and Rob clearing our path in almost biblical fashion then I'd probably get swept away, but everyone stands aside to let them pass.

My head is spinning as the next train pulls haltingly away, juddering like the driver keeps applying the breaks for no reason other than to make me feel worse. That all-too-familiar watery sensation rises in my mouth and I try to swallow it back, but the train lurches forward again. Bad timing.

Hunched in my seat, I vomit some sort of terrible frothy liquid all over the floor, splashing my boots and the shoes of the man sitting opposite. He pretends not to notice, desperately avoiding eye contact.

The train picks up speed, going too fast like the driver's doing this on purpose too, bouncing us around in our seats, thundering faster and faster like we're on a fucking fairground ride. I hunch forward again, trying not to puke while watching my alcoholic expulsions work their way down the carriage in the gaps between the wooden slatted floors. It's probably the reason that tube trains don't have those wooden floors anymore.

Eventually we reach the station at Leicester Square and the two skinheads stride on ahead, leaving us behind. Doubtless they have better things to do than play nursemaid to me, and if only I'd known it was that easy to get rid of them I would have thrown up sooner. Neil leads me off the train towards the escalators. I can stand, albeit in wobbly legs, but I need pointing in the right direction. He tells the ticket inspector to fuck off and tries to drag me past the ticket booth, but I stop, stupidly proffering a ticket that's three days out of date. We haven't got valid tickets. I learned very quickly that no one bothers to buy tickets, this being pre-CCTV and jaws-of-death barriers. Even a ticket inspector is a rarity.

Neil tugs at my sleeve again, to get me moving, but I fall over, landing in a dishevelled heap at the inspector's feet and causing a blockage as people attempt to get by. We're beginning to draw a crowd, half from people shoving to get past, others just stopping to gape at this sorry spectacle. My legs are useless and I can't get up.

"Fugoff!" I blurt, a helpless cripple as Neil tries to drag me to my feet. "Leeme 'lone."

"I fuckin' *will* leave you here if you don't get your shit together," Neil snarls, apparently able to understand what I'm saying.

He gives my arm one final yank and I sprawl forward, somehow back on my feet but unable to stop the momentum as I crash through the gathering crowd of spectators. All the while, the inspector is pointlessly demanding a valid ticket, but people are moving quickly out of my path, fearful of vomit and flailing arms, making a path to the exit. Almost blind with drunkenness and fatigue, I see daylight filtering in from the street and I make a dash for freedom.

The short walk to Trafalgar Square is a blur, as is most of the morning. I remember cleaning the puke off my boots in the fountain and harassing tourists, but not a great deal else. And then, somehow, it's midday and Neil suggests that we pay the Hare Krishnas a visit to see about some free food. He pronounces the name as if they were part of the Great Train Robbery, East End gangsters: Ronnie Biggs and Harry Krishna.

We head north towards Oxford Street. I stop outside a huge department store to check my hair in the reflection of the window and the security man springs to attention, making it clear that we're not welcome inside. Apparently our money isn't as good as everyone else's. Probably because we haven't got any. To be fair, I look rather the worse for wear. I straighten a sagging spike and move on.

Neil does the talking when we reach the Krishna place, but his powers of persuasion and that smooth – no doubt forked – tongue are not needed. They remember us from yesterday and the deal still stands; if we sit through one of their prayer meetings or whatever they are, they will feed us. We clump noisily up a narrow staircase and one of the Krishnas requests that we take our boots off outside a room at the top. After a short argument and an assurance that no one will steal our boots, we comply, and I'm almost sick again because of the overwhelming stench from Neil's socks. He need not worry about theft. No sane person would go near anything that had come into contact with his rancid feet. But then, I know very little about the Krishna faith; maybe a pair of socks that can walk on their own would be considered a holy relic.

We enter a small room, half a dozen or so people already sitting, with varying degrees of success, in the lotus position.

"Fuckin' hippies," Neil mutters contemptuously.

I throw him a glance that says, "shut up or we won't get fed" and we take a cushion each from a small pile in the corner, joining the fucking hippies on the floor. The room is as I would have imagined, if I'd bothered to think about it; vaguely Indian-looking, with ornate drapes and a strong smell of incense, possibly to disguise the smell of feet. I get comfortable on the cushion, sitting cross-legged but avoiding any yoga positions that I might get stuck in. I have never been supple, barely able to touch my toes, and I see no reason to even attempt such things now that I don't have a PE teacher bellowing abuse at me about my gymnastic inadequacies. Neil sits down noisily in a space behind me and we wait as a couple more people enter the room and take their places.

It's quiet in here, no trace of the hustle of the West End outside, and I become dimly aware of my senses, the aches and pains of abuse, the sore throat from throwing up, the ringing ears from last night's gig, already a lifetime ago. I get another whiff of Neil's odorous feet, still not entirely masked by the incense, and realize that my own feet, while not actually stinking, are in need of some serious attention. With my boots off for the first time in many, many hours, my feet throb with relief. The palms of my hands are grazed from falling over, as is my elbow. My stomach grumbles with hunger. If this is body awareness you can stick it up your arse.

Someone is talking, a vague murmur drifting from the front of the room. I think they might have been talking for a while, but I wasn't paying attention and can't be bothered to start now. I don't have the slightest interest in Krishna, at least not today. I'm just here for the food. It's a soothing voice, though, an unintrusive, reassuring mantra, and again I drift off into my own world, enjoying this brief respite from the obnoxious duties of punk rock. I notice my heartbeat and the rhythm of my breathing, slow and deep. Inhale. Exhale. Inhale. Exhale. The calming words flow over me in waves. Inhale. Exhale. Inhale... Jesus, what's that fucking smell?

Behind me, Neil almost splits his sides trying not to laugh. Clearly, he has farted, and it's not just any common or garden fart; this is the fart of a man who eats from dustbins, a putrid, eggy stench at hangs in the air like a foul, black cloud, and could be used with apocalyptic success for chemical warfare. It really is eye-wateringly rank! He snorts, either trying not to laugh or trying not to breathe in his own foetid fumes. Good God, it's disgusting!

Even though he's behind me, I can sense his shoulders bobbing up and down with mirth. In case I hadn't noticed – and how could I possibly *not* have noticed? – he pokes me in the back with a warm, sticky toe to alert me of the genius of his backside. Despite myself, I get an uncontrollable fit of the giggles that gets worse the more I try not to laugh. Tears stream down my face. Although, to be fair, this might be because of the smell of untreated sewage emanating from Neil's unwashed anus.

Always one to take a joke too far, Neil lifts himself onto one buttock and squeezes out another revolting retort, this time an audible quack, like a cartoon duck whistle. He lets out a small weep of delight, and with renewed vigour our shoulders bob up and down, like boats in choppy water. Fuck's sake, this one's worse! Surely there are laws against such effluence? I'm pretty sure it's mentioned in the Geneva Convention!

Despite some sharp looks from the hippies we manage to sit through the whole meeting without getting thrown out. When it's over we traipse back outside and retrieve our boots, then, while the hippies disperse, Neil gets chatting to one of the Krishnas about the possibilities of us getting fed. They are understandably reluctant to invite us into their restaurant, but we are eventually presented with a bowl of food each and left to eat it sitting on the stairs. I feel a tinge of guilt that we behaved so foolishly when these people have welcomed us into their world without judgement. All they asked was that we sit and listen and we couldn't even do that. I attempt a grateful smile, but Neil just grunts and takes his food, not even bothering to make eye contact. He pokes the offering with a suspicious fork before taking a mouthful.

"Just making sure these bits ain't rat shit," he explains, prodding a piece of brown rice.

This is rich coming from someone who happily will eat three-day-old McDonald's out of a bin, but I let it pass. I was actually checking mine to make sure our hosts hadn't spat in it as repayment for Neil's noxious gasses and our subsequent glee. Can't say I'd blame them if they did, but there appears to be nothing more offensive in the bowl than some rather bland rice-based dish.

"This is fuckin' 'orrible," Neil grumbles through a large mouthful. "Wouldn't feed it to a pig."

Admittedly, it's not to my taste, but it's the only thing I've eaten in days and it's free, so I keep quiet, while Neil keeps complaining. Ungrateful cunt.

"Fuckin' slop," Neil continues, but with rather less conviction since he's nearly finished and is eyeing my bowl, like a lion watching a three-legged zebra. Or a dung beetle eyeing up shit.

I force another mouthful down, but my brain seems to have forgotten how to deal with food, regarding it now as a foreign body. After a few more mouthfuls, each swallowed like a child taking medicine, I give up and hand the bowl to Neil, who greedily shovels the contents into his face. I wait for him quietly, avoiding eye contact with our hosts in case one of them decides to talk to me. When he's done, Neil tries unsuccessfully to wangle another helping. So much for slop.

Back out on the street we wander aimlessly for a while, looking for something to do. I'm tempted to get on the road again, but it's too late in the day to go anywhere. The Banshees are playing in Bristol and doubtless my obnoxious companion can get us in for 'nuffin', but there's no guarantee we'd get there, especially since he hasn't changed his clothes or washed himself since the last time we hitched anywhere. Besides which, I kind of promised Corrine that I'd go back to her place, and I've left my sleeping bag there. Instead, we head for the nearest off-licence and I buy a pack of cigarettes while Neil is stealing a bottle of cider.

A new plan is hatched: head to the park, drink Neil's cider, and then ditch the cunt and go back to Vauxhall for a night of filthy sex. Perfect. Instead we walk out of the off-licence and straight into Joe and Rob.

CHAPTER EIGHTEEN

BITTER EXPERIENCE HAS taught me to avoid Leicester Square like the plague. Apparently the place got a facelift – extensively remodelled and refurbished – for the 2012 Olympics, after the council rather belatedly realised that it wasn't safe for tourists, but you can pretty much guarantee that it's still a dump. By day you can visit, should you be so singularly lacking imagination, the world's biggest Lego store. By night you can see pissheads fighting each other and throwing up on the pavement. You can only polish a turd so much, so I shouldn't think it's changed much.

But still this is a vast improvement. In the late '70s and early-to-mid '80s the north end of the square was usually infested with skinheads, horrible street rats with bad facial tattoos and glue bags. And they were the nicer ones. Mostly because they were too fucked up to cause problems, their glazed eyes rarely becoming aware of potential prey, their wobbly legs unable to carry them in more than a shuffle, much less give chase. It was the others you had to watch out for, psychos like Joe who would blatantly fleece any young punk who was unfortunate enough to encounter them. They'd demand a cigarette or some spare change, and then when you said you hadn't got any they'd go through your pockets and take whatever they could find. Daylight robbery in a very literal sense.

Only a few months earlier, I had travelled up to London with a friend to see the legendary Apocalypse Now show with Discharge, Exploited, Anti Pasti, Chron Gen, and the Anti Nowhere League, and we found ourselves in that exact situation, having accidentally strayed into the square. Luckily for us, a passing cop witnessed the entire thing and forced the skinhead to return our tickets and money, but it was unpleasant, to say the least, feeling so helpless.

It probably sounds stupid to have tolerated such behaviour, cowardly even, but there really wasn't a great deal you could do about it, apart from stay the fuck away from them. Years later, I heard an unlikely interview with Crass frontman Steve Ignorant and the self-styled 'godfather of Oi' Garry Bushell in which Bushell asked why the punks didn't fight back more often. To which Ignorant pointed out that Crass fans were usually the kid with the gimpy leg or the runt of the litter, and they were up against hardened hooligans. I'm paraphrasing, and punk had and still has its fair share of nutters, but it's not far from the truth. Not that I have a gimpy leg, but when you're built like a coat hanger, 120lbs soaking wet with a studded leather jacket, you don't have a lot of options. If some fucking nutcase wants to go through your pockets then you let him, at least until you've put on a few pounds and learned to defend yourself.

Today is different, however. Today Neil and I are guests of the fucking nutcase, who seems, inexplicably, to have taken a liking to us. There's a gang of about ten skinheads in the square, and Joe is clearly the alpha male, if only because Rob is too dim-witted to claim the title for himself. Together they offer us protection by simple virtue of the fact that we are seen to be with them. Unfortunately, we are also guilty by association and, worse still, complicit by our actions, laughing at their stupid racist jokes and pretending to fit in so we don't get a kicking, ever aware of Joe's fondness for violence and that his mood can change in a heartbeat.

Admittedly, Rob is quite funny as he lollops after some scabby-looking "National Front pigeons", wildly flapping his arms about and yelling "Lookatdacoons! Lookatdacoons!", but it would still be funny without the racism. And it's not as if I can use the tired defence that "some of my best friends are black"; I don't really know any black people. I just laugh because I haven't got the guts to tell him to shut up. The irony being that I'm not even sure that Rob is the racist he purports to be, just a knucklehead seeking approval. How quickly we reduce ourselves to the lowest common denominator.

Which, in no small way, is what was wrong with the Oi movement.

Not that all the bands were racist by any means, some of them actively fighting against racism. But a few were, and so were a large number of the fans, and too many people tolerated it. Fearful of violence, many talented people just abandoned the scene completely. Granted, just as many fought back, but it was hardly a fun night out, and more about being tough than having any talent for music. There were some great bands in amongst the rubbish, but why risk a beating to see them?

Despite the evidence of his soiled swastika T-shirt I sense that Neil is equally uncomfortable. He may be many things, not least a shifty, thieving cunt, but he has no sympathy for Nazis. Hell, he can barely muster sympathy for Hare Krishnas, and they *fed* him. He's far too lazy and self-centred to be sympathetic to the 'master race'. We exchange 'let's get the fuck out of here' glances and make our excuses, leaving them to their 'nigger' and 'Paki' jokes.

A short walk and we're back in Trafalgar Square. Again. Harassing tourists and poncing money until we have enough for a bottle of cider each. Ponce, drink, repeat. Watching stupid tourists feed the stupid pigeons. Free to do whatever we want, but with nothing to do. Various punks drift in and out of the square, a few familiar faces and a few new friends, some of whom would remain so for years. Strangely, given that I often can't remember people that I met last week, I can distinctly recall meeting some of them for the first time. I was going to tell a tale or two about them, but most are dead now and their tales are not always happy. Drugs, violence, and prison. Spit, Sniper, Andy, Black Luke, Major, Mark Shark, Paul, Tracy, Sarah, Nicki, Android, Pus… The list is depressingly long. So many gone so young. Just kids.

One face that stands out, though, is Dragon Tim, so called because he had – still has – a large dragon tattooed on the side of his head. Back then he seemed like a giant, over six feet tall, with a black Mohican adding another six inches or so, but he was always a welcome sight and particularly useful if it all kicked off. Indeed, he worked the door at the Marquee for several years and security at the 100 Club, his fearsome appearance serving to stop many fights before they'd even started. We would later fight side by side on numerous occasions, but he had – and has – a gentle soul, a peacekeeper rather than a troublemaker. We're still friends today, and he should probably write his own book, his life being infinitely more interesting than mine. He's some sort of guru these days, white robed, living in a jungle somewhere, his face a maze of laughter lines. It's good to know that some of the old crew survived.

He hangs out with us for a while, a magnet for tourist cameras, but he has an actual job, working on a stall of some sort by day, selling badges, so he has no need to be poncing money. He's just passing through.

"I'm thinking of fucking off out of London," I tell Neil, when Tim leaves.

"Oh yeah?" he brightens. "Where to?"

"Dunno."

We get some more cider.

Some hours later we are still in the square. Bored and drunk. I should have gone to Bristol for the Banshees show. Should have gone anywhere but here. This is confirmed by the sudden appearance of Raggetty being carried across the square like some wounded soldier from the battlefield, a grubby-looking punk on either side of him. Indeed, 'sudden' is entirely the wrong word, because I have never seen Raggetty do anything sudden, except perhaps suddenly falling through a table full of drinks, or suddenly being at the centre of a fight that he has no idea he started. I have rarely seen him walk unaided and today he is, if anything, even more of a mess than usual. Slumped between the two punks, he is apparently incapable of putting one foot in front of the other, just dragged along on scuffed boots, legs bent at the knees, his head hanging forward as if searching the ground for dogends, drugs, money, who knows what. As the punks draw to a halt in front of us, Raggetty struggles to lift his head so he can see who they're talking to.

"Alright, Raggetty?"

There is a brief glimmer of recognition as he manages to get both his head and his eyes to point in my direction.

"Having fun?"

His top lip twitches, creasing into what, for Raggetty, passes as a smile. Terrible yellow teeth. An affirmative. Raggetty is having fun. Granted, he probably thinks he's at a gig, but who am I to shatter this illusion? I'm almost tempted to ask him what band he thinks he's watching, but he appears unable to speak in anything more than a mumbled grunt. Christ knows what he's taken, but since it's often a large combination of coloured pills that no one knows the name of, topped off with Tuinal, Mogadon, and methylated spirits, there seems little point in asking. Side effects may include being Raggetty. The fact that he's still breathing is a small miracle. More so that he's apparently still alive at the time of writing this.

I watch the two punks carefully lower him to the ground and rest him against a plinth bearing the statue of someone I've never heard of. But I offer no assistance in case it's interpreted as wanting to take responsibility for him. Raggetty is so fucked up most of the time that he has to be carried – or at the very least led – everywhere he goes, and the last thing you want is to be left in charge of his welfare. He's little more than a dirty, spiky-haired skeleton in a leather jacket, concentration camp thin, so weight is not a problem even if it is dead weight. The main problem is that his appearance so offends people that they feel compelled to attack him pretty much everywhere he goes. And, of course, he's too fucked up to defend himself so you end up fighting his battles for him.

One time in particular, someone had thought it wise to take him to a gig downstairs at the Clarendon in Hammersmith, a small and grotty pub/music venue beneath the legendary Klub Foot. They'd been dragging the bastard around for hours and so left him, crumpled and dribbling, on a wooden chair, while they went to watch the band. When they returned there was a heated argument going on between punks and bouncers, that seemed to centre around the table they'd left Raggetty at.

"Get that cunt out of here!" insisted one of the bouncers, pointing at our comatose cohort.

And there, indeed, was Raggetty, sitting in a pool of his own piss.

A foul-mouthed and fiery punk girl called Scottish Katie and a kid called Moggy – named after his own fondness for Mogadon – struggled to get him to his feet as the row got more heated, and with a rake-thin arm around each of their shoulders, they dragged him towards the exit. The bouncer wasn't content with them following his instructions, however, and he stood in front of the door, barring their way while yelling at them to vacate the premises.

At this point, Raggetty slipped from their grasp and slid to the sticky carpeted floor. They wrestled him upright again, took a step to the door, and then, suddenly, the bouncer lost control and punched Raggetty hard in the face. It was then that Ken stepped into the fray.

Ken is a fearsome bastard, and I use the present tense because he is still very much alive and still quite terrifying, now a high-ranking hench-man for some ultra-right organisation or other. I shall refrain from using his surname because I only live 6,000 miles away from him, which is rather too close for comfort. But to give you some idea of his reputation, let's just say that he used to switch between being a punk and a skinhead in much the same way that the wind changes direction. This was not, as was often the case with others, because his friends had changed with the whims of fashion from one week to the next. Rather, it would occur in a matter of seconds, just to even up the sides. One night at the Rainbow Theatre in Finsbury Park there was a huge battle where skinheads out-numbered punks about four to one, and so, despite all evidence to the contrary, Ken announced that he was now a punk, and promptly started battering skinheads.

On the night of the Clarendon incident Ken was a punk and therefore slightly, but only very slightly, more likely to be on our side. Like a flash, he stepped between Raggetty and the bouncer and suggested, with great directness and very few syllables, that he should pick on someone his own size. With practised ease, the bouncer, clearly having more sense than we'd credited him with, then produced a baseball bat from behind a chair and smashed Ken in the face with it. Ken reeled for a second, more surprised than hurt, and then all hell broke loose.

I look at Raggetty now, slumped against the plinth like a badly tied sack of toothpicks, his eyes glazed, barely conscious. Fuck that! I'm not getting stuck with him today. I turn to Neil, slipping him a sly cigarette and lighting one for myself, not wanting to lose half the pack by doing it openly and having every fucker take one.

"We should fuck off," I murmur, nodding towards Raggetty.

Neil nods, but in the instant that we turn our backs the other two punks have gone, vanished into thin air like a couple of sneaky magicians. I scan the square in case they've just wandered off to hassle tourists for a moment, but there's no sign of them. Bastards! In this perverse and never-ending game of pass the parcel, the music has stopped on us.

"Maybe we can straighten him out a bit," I suggest without much hope.

Unfortunately, leaving him here is not an option and we don't even voice the thought. Raggetty might be a complete pain in the arse, but there for the grace of the wrong combination of drugs and alcohol go us. We've all been there, if not quite so regularly as this cunt. Only this morning I was cleaning puke off my boots, and if not for Neil I might still be lost on the London Underground.

I vaguely remember that Raggetty lives in a squat in Campbell Buildings, but I'm not exactly sure where that it, and the few times I've been there it was a horror show of junkies and roaming boneheads. Corrine's place is also out of the question. She's had quite enough uninvited guests. Instead, we drag him over to the fountains, propping him up while we splash water on his face. Which makes him slightly cleaner but no more coherent. His sickly white face and tattooed neck protrude from his leather jacket like that of a cancerous tortoise from a rotten shell. A thin line of drool hangs from his lower lip. Neil starts going through his pockets, not, as I first thought, to find some sort of ID or something with an address, but to see if he's got any drugs. With the exception of some scabies lotion and a solitary safety pin his pockets are empty.

And so it would seem that we are stuck with Raggetty. There are no more punks in the square, no one to palm him off on. And, worse still, the last of the cider has gone. The sun sets late on an English summer, but I'm guessing it's only a few hours away. The heat of the day is fading and so am I. I don't want to deal with this shit.

"Fuck it," I tell Neil. "You watch him for a minute and I'll go and get some more cider. You want some smokes?"

To be fair, I said I was going to get cider, not that I was bringing any back. And I asked if he wanted cigarettes, I didn't say I was going to get him any.

I never saw Neil again.

CHAPTER NINETEEN

HOW QUICKLY WE learn the ways of the guttersnipe. Only a week ago I knew nothing of the art of poncing, and yet here I am making more in a day than I get paid for a full week of working in a factory. Easy money. Fifty pence or more per picture. Although technically it's a modelling job of sorts, posing for tourists. The true art of poncing is more about asking for spare change and doing nothing in return. Begging – occasionally with menaces – which is something I am not prepared to do, not least because I'm not very menacing.

I have also learned that, despite all the evidence to the contrary, Raggetty probably doesn't have scabies. A lot of punks carry scabies lotion as a deterrent to cops who might want to rummage through their pockets, the thought of catching an infestation of nasty mites making them reluctant to continue their search for whatever the hell it is they're looking for. Unfortunately, I learn this *after* I've been searched for no apparent reason, but it's a lesson worth remembering. Especially since the cop escorts me to an old-fashioned police box and all but strip-searches me. He's polite enough about it, almost apologetic when I'm polite in return, but there's still no need to be dropping my trousers just to satisfy his inquisitive nature.

Having made a lazy start to the day, fucking all morning and preening our hair, Corrine and I headed, inevitably, to Trafalgar Square to drink and hustle money. It's another gloriously hot day and business is brisk. It helps that we're happy to kiss on demand for the cameras, and there are worse ways to make a living. Tax-free. Flexible hours. No boss to answer to. And what it lacks in promotion prospects is more than made up by the fact that you can get pissed on the job. It beats working in a fucking factory, that's for sure.

For the first time since my journey began, it occurs to me that it will soon come to an end. One more week and I'll have to go back to that wretched place. The same mindless job day after day, staring at the paint flaking off the walls, the radio endlessly repeating insipid hits as I work at some godforsaken metal-pressing machine. Many are the days that it's given me a black eye when my concentration has lapsed and the handle has smacked me in the face. Many more are the days that I've wanted to burn the place to the ground.

And this is to say nothing of the long walk to and from work, frequently in the pissing rain. Not that I mind the walk, to be honest. What I resent is getting paid a pound a week less than I'd get on the dole, and the fact that I'm supposed to be grateful for it. With millions unemployed, I'm 'lucky' to have a job at all no matter how soul-destroying, no matter that there seems to be no way out. The job centre, with its near-empty shelves, is open nine-to-five, Monday to Friday, so how the fuck are you supposed to look for a different job? I've run away from home before, first at around nine or ten years old, and again at fifteen, but today it occurs to me that I don't actually *have* to go back. Who would bother looking for me if I never returned? What do I have to go back *to*? What if I just stayed in London?

My reverie is interrupted by Corrine legging after some Japanese tourists who were taking sneaky pictures of us, and explaining to them in no uncertain terms that such things are not free. She comes back two quid better off. Four hours' work in the factory. We must be due a lunch break by now. Liquid lunch, of course.

Perhaps strangely, at a time when punks are generally seen as targets for violence or abuse, we encounter no hostility, just curiosity. We chat for a while with a middle-aged couple from Iowa who have never seen punks before, then share our cider with an old lady from San Francisco who tells us all about beatniks, which seem to me to be hippies reciting bad poetry. Doubtless it helps that Neil's not around with his swastika T-shirt and his finger up his nose, or that there is no one openly sniffing glue but, still, I'm pleasantly surprised by how friendly everyone is. It makes a nice change from being threatened.

When evening draws near we head north to Wardour Street, where the UK Subs and Charge are playing at the legendary Marquee club, another great venue that has sadly bitten the dust and is now a cigar shop or some such bollocks. The original venue, opened in 1958, was on Oxford Street and mostly hosted jazz bands, but between 1964 and 1988, after relocating to the Wardour Street premises, just about everyone who's anyone played there; Pink Floyd, Hendrix, Rolling Stones, The Who, Led Zeppelin, Bowie, Queen, Motörhead, Sex Pistols, the Damned, U2, Metallica… The list is almost endless. The giants of rock 'n' roll. At the end of which, a commission discovered that all those years of loud bands making the walls vibrate had caused the building to subside and that it would need to be demolished, which I suppose is a fitting end.

The club relocated again, to a bigger venue at the north end of Charing Cross Road, and hosted yet more classic bands, like Alice In Chains, Poison Idea, Pantera, Faith No More, Sepultura, The Prodigy, and more. But while it was a great club, it never had quite the same filthy ambience as Wardour Street, with its infamous beer-sticky carpet and sweat running down the walls, a thousand or more people jammed into a place that was meant to hold less than half that number. Apparently, the attendance record was 1,400 for Bon Scott era AC/DC, packed in like greased sardines.

The Charing Cross Road venue went tits up in 1996, and the club's famous name was slapped on various woefully unworthy establishments, each one a little more sanitised and a little more soulless than the last. Clean floors and clean toilets. One of them was in a fucking shopping centre. Its final location was in Leicester Square, from 2004 until 2008 – or 2006, depending on which website you believe. I never went there, and I can't find any pictures of it online, but it sounds horrible. State of the art. Missing the point. Someone still owns the name, but that's about it.

Pretty much opposite the Marquee on Wardour Street was a sketchy pub called The Intrepid Fox, which I now discover has a rich history dating back as far as 1784, until it was closed in 2006 to make way for a burger joint. I wish I was making this up. Along with a place called The Ship – surprisingly still there and virtually unchanged – it was the nearest watering hole to the club and so tended to be packed with whoever was going to the gig, which, on this night, was wall-to-wall punks and a couple of stray skinheads, too few in number to be any bother.

No one ever checked ID at the Fox and at least half of us were under the legal drinking age, all acting like it's nothing special. And maybe it was nothing special to the others, but when you come from a village with about three pubs, all equally unwelcoming, it's pretty cool to be in a place that's packed with your own kind, stinking of patchouli and beer, wall-to-wall leather jackets and spiky hair. Back home, there's a choice of two places where the local toughs will kick your face in, and the oldies pub where your stepdad drinks. None of them are known for their love of punk rockers. All of them require proof that you're old enough to drink alcohol.

After several pints in the Fox, we head over to the Marquee, already pissed, and I remember drinking more at the bar back. Unfortunately, I don't remember much else. Charge were a decent band, with a cracking single called *King's Cross*, and I saw them many times, but this show doesn't ring any bells. And, Christ, I must have seen the Subs a hundred times or more over the years, but, again, nothing specific springs to mind. They had numerous chart hits and were able to fill much bigger venues than the Marquee at that time, so it was undoubtedly a special gig, and one from which I emerged sweaty and smiling from the pit, but the details are gone. Old cunt.

Although sometimes maybe that's not a bad thing. It means there were no fights that night, no blood on the dance floor, just a good gig. Or maybe the memory has been eclipsed by what happened afterwards.

The shows always finish early at the Marquee, curfew at eleven, because the top two floors are occupied by printers who work nights. Corrine and I loiter at the bar after the show, and it's not long before we're joined by none other than UK Subs singer Charlie Harper and the Damned's guitarist Captain Sensible. Which is a big deal when you're seventeen and come from the Isle of Wight. Punk royalty, if there ever was such a thing. I'd met Sensible before, briefly, when my high school band, Thin Red Line, somehow ended up opening for them at a rare Isle of Wight show, but this is different. Hanging out. Corrine is friends with Harper – probably a little more than friends, as I later discovered – so it's not like we're just fans, lingering around for autographs. There's a couple of other punks, Harper's friends, a girl who seems to be with Sensible, and no one seems in a hurry to kick us out while we finish our drinks.

When finally it's clear that the staff are locking the place up for the night, we head outside, half a dozen of us ambling up Wardour Street. There's some talk of maybe finding a club that's open late, but options are apparently limited, too far away or too trendy. The pubs are already closed and the streets are empty. Instead, Harper and Sensible get into a conversation about going to a studio tonight to record something, a spur of the moment session. Get some beers in, jam some tunes, and see what happens. I can hardly believe my ears. Punk rock history in the making. The chance to see how it all happens! A dream come true! Maybe I'll even get to do some backing vocals, but I'd be more than happy to sit quietly in the corner and just watch the magic.

They're still discussing the plan, knocking ideas around, as we wait for the last train on an otherwise empty platform at Tottenham Court Road station. And then Sensible nods in our direction, me and Corrine and Harper's two friends.

"Let's get rid of the dead weight," he says.

And to his eternal credit Charlie does just that, and we leave Sensible behind.

CHAPTER TWENTY

I SEEM TO remember that Charlie Harper's flat was somewhere on the Stockwell Road. Maybe he still lives there. It turned out that we'd missed the last train, so we jump in a black cab, Charlie, Corrine and I, a blur of magical London streets passing the window. It was a sensation that never grew stale, even years after moving to the city, a truly enchanting place by night and into the early morning. In a different lifetime, I loved coming home as the sun was beginning to rise, the Ecstasy wearing off as we gazed out upon street life and street lights. But this was my first time in a black cab – and indeed my last for many years, since penniless punks take night buses, or walk if they've missed the last tube – so it was particularly special, not least because of the company. So much is lost over time, forgotten or mundane, but not this.

Any sense of disappointment I felt towards Sensible was gone in an instant. Ironically, he and Charlie finally got around to recording an EP together in 2013 and it's wholly unremarkable, so maybe they could have done with some 'dead weight' after all. Either way, it's pretty far from the historic punk collaboration that it should be. And, either way, I still love the Damned and the UK Subs.

But I digress. The lack of disappointment wasn't due to a dodgy single yet to come, but to a sense of awe at being in Charlie Harper's home. Looking back, it was hardly a penthouse suite, but at seventeen it was a palace, plush-carpeted, the walls lined with various framed discs commemorating outstanding record sales, all of which I owned. Me and thousands of others.

The Subs were always bothering the charts, always on *Top of the Pops*, and here's Charlie handing me a beer and giving me the guided tour. Granted, he was probably shagging my new girlfriend, but I was too naive to know. Even after I'd been tucked up in a nice comfy bed in the spare room. On my own. It didn't occur to me for years. Besides, it wasn't entirely clear what the relationship status was between myself and Corrine. We didn't talk about it, just hung out and fucked, both knowing that I wasn't staying. That was enough and maybe all it should ever have been.

The next day we get the tube back to her place and do just that. Sundays used to be the day for big gigs at the Lyceum, but I guess there was nothing good on. Out of curiosity I scoured the internet, but there's no sign of any shows, good or otherwise. Frederick's Of Hollywood introduced thong underwear to the United States that day, but it seems that no one played the Lyceum. It's only been a week since the Killing Joke show. Already another lifetime.

We stay in the next day, too, Pink Floyd drifting on a hot, sticky breeze through the open window. I have no idea where it's coming from, but it's not unwelcome. *Wish You Were Here* and *Shine On You Crazy Diamond* over and over, from afternoon until early evening when Corrine gets ready for work at the Rock Garden. There's a band called the Mo-dettes playing, but they're not my kinda thing – an all-girl 'post punk' band who had a minor hit or two and whose bassist Jane Crockford gained some notoriety for trying to bite Shane McGowan's ear off at a Clash gig – so I sit at the bar while Corrine feeds me free beer. I can claim to have seen the band, but not much else.

And so comes Tuesday. Another blissful day of doing nothing, but with it the vague notion that I should be doing something. Moving on. Going somewhere. It's not as if there was ever a plan, but if there had been then this was not it. The Banshees are playing Cardiff today, too far to hitch with any certainty of actually getting there, but the gig guide says they're doing Gloucester tomorrow, only a few hours away if I get lucky with rides. There seems no reason not to go.

Until a few years ago I kept a list of every gig I ever went to, every band I'd ever seen. Hundreds of gigs, thousands of bands, some of them hundreds of times. According to this list, I went to see Chelsea, Chron

Gen and Lemon Kittens at the 100 Club on Oxford Street that Tuesday night. But, again, it stirs no particular memories. Chelsea had – and have – a few great songs, although I always found their anthem *Right To Work* somewhat baffling, since most of their audience didn't want to work and went out of their way to be unemployable. Likewise, Chron Gen were a reasonable enough band, if nothing life-changing. Fuck knows who Lemon Kittens were, but the name's not exactly promising. Not that there haven't been countless other memorable shows at the 100 Club – every Tuesday and Thursday was punk night – I just don't recall this one.

So fuck it, why not throw in some history? You can always skip to the next chapter if you want to get back to the random violence and horrible nutcases.

According to their website the 100 Club opened as a live music venue on October 24th 1942, originally a restaurant called Macks, which was hired out as the Feldman Swing Club. Apparently the jitterbug was popular and banned at most other clubs, and people would go there to jitter as the bombs fell on London during the Second World War. And we thought punk rock was dangerous.

By 1948 it had become the London Jazz Club, and for the most part I fucking hate jazz, so you can look that up yourselves. Suffice to say, jazz was probably still considered to be the devil's music and downfall of humanity, so it's cool that the club was hosting that music, and continues to do so.

It became the 100 Club in 1964 – so named because of its location at 100 Oxford Street – and hosted blues legends like BB King, Muddy Waters, and Bo Diddley, not to mention such giants as The Who, The Kinks, and The Animals. But the place went through tough times in the '70s with economic depression leading to a three-day working week, during which time electricity was shut off between 6pm and 9pm. Everywhere! I'm guessing hospitals and the like were exempt, but I was too young to even notice, too busy listening to Slade, Bowie, and Sweet, and, much as I hate to admit it, Gary Glitter. We won't dwell on that loathsome piece of shit – currently serving 16 years in prison, and hopefully deceased by the time you read this – but it is, in hindsight, not a little ironic that glam rock, with all its trappings of decadence, was the biggest musical phenomenon at the time.

Maybe it was a form of escapism, the protest songs of the '60s having failed to bring about revolution, peaceful or otherwise. Certainly there was little rebellion in glam rock beyond Slade misspelling song titles to annoy your parents. Although, again in hindsight, the gender bending and androgyny of Bowie and T. Rex was a statement in itself. Big boys don't cry, and they sure as fuck don't wear lipstick. It was less than a decade before, in 1967, that homosexuality was decriminalised in the UK, and you could still get a kicking for being a 'poof' if you wore an earring in the wrong ear.

Then along comes punk rock and, again, the 100 Club was host to a genre of music that was unwelcome pretty much everywhere else. September 1976 saw the first punk festival, featuring, over two days, the Clash, the Damned, Sex Pistols, the Banshees, Vibrators and more, all of them unsigned, and, despite Sid Vicious lobbing a beer glass at the stage, blinding a girl in one eye, punk made its home there for the next eight years or so. It's still a home from home, albeit to a lesser extent, and pretty much unchanged. Same shitty dressing room. Same paint job. Same stupid pillar in the middle of the dance floor. Bless 'em.

But here's the weird part…

Well, perhaps not weird, but certainly a beautifully odd twist of fate.

In 2010 it was announced that the 100 Club was closing down. Drowning in debt, losing £100,000 a year due to soaring rent, it was destined to go the way of all the other legendary venues. Various big names stepped in to help – Mick Jagger, Liam Gallagher, Paul McCartney, who played a benefit show there – but with a capacity of just 300 they'd have to charge £100 a ticket and sell the place out every night of the year just to break even. Something like that. Math was never a strong point. Granted, any of those three musicians could have bought the place outright and run it as a tax loss or something, but instead it was up to punk rock to come to the rescue. Sort of…

From around the end of 1981 until maybe '85, I was the singer – if you can call it such – for a punk band called Soldiers Of Destruction, and we played the 100 Club countless times opening for the likes of GBH, Exploited, English Dogs, and Vice Squad. Even headlined the place once. The band fizzled out and I hadn't seen our drummer Rick Copcutt in years, finally running into him in LA. He was still every inch the punk rocker, tattooed neck and all, but he was now vice president/general manager of Converse.

Anyway, one day he's being driven past the 100 Club and happens to read a newspaper article about its impeding closure. "Fuck that!" he says to himself. "I grew up there!" And he gets the car to pull over, presumably in the bus lane since there's nowhere to park on Oxford Street. The doors were open, and he went downstairs into the club, where he found the manager at his desk, looking, as one might expect, utterly glum.

"I heard you're closing down," said Rick.

"Fucking vultures are closing in already," replied the manager, or something to that effect. Upon which our hero revealed his true identity, not as some tattooed oik looking for souvenirs but as a tattooed oik with access to some serious money. What's more, his idea was to keep the place intact, rather than covering it in Converse logos and tacky banners. If memory serves, one of the few stipulations was that Converse could put their own gigs on for two weeks of the year. Free gigs, if I remember correctly.

And so it was that the 100 Club was saved from becoming yet another Starbucks, or whatever vile fate lay in store. Ironically, Soldiers Of Destruction were banned from playing there after a particularly drunken and unruly performance opening for English Dogs. I'm told that ban has now been lifted.

CHAPTER TWENTY-ONE

THERE IS AN old English nursery rhyme, apparently first published in 1844, perhaps much older.

Doctor Foster went to Gloucester

In a shower of rain

He stepped in a puddle

Right up to his middle

And never went there again.

There are various explanations as to who the good Doctor was and what he might have been doing in Gloucester, but one thing's for sure, he had the right idea. Gloucester is a shithole and no one in their right mind would go there twice.

Despite a relatively low population, it had, between October 2014 and September 2015, the third highest murder rate in England and Wales. Which is obviously not including those committed by two of its most infamous former residents, Fred and Rosemary West, who, between 1967 and 1987, killed at least 12 girls, including their own daughter. According to Google Maps, I was just three minutes from their Cromwell Street residence when I went to Gloucester. I may even have walked past the place – unremarkable in every way apart from its corpse-filled back yard – on my way to the venue. All I remember is that it was raining. Grey skies in a grey town.

Corrine saw me off from Victoria Coach Station that morning, waving at me through the window as the coach belched out its foul exhaust fumes. No tears, but perhaps a moment of melancholy. I saw her again just twice;

one time about three months later, when I showed up uninvited on her doorstep looking for a place to crash after hitching back to London from Guildford, which she provided with good grace, despite having company. The next time was maybe six years after that, when I bumped into her at a club called Dingwalls in Camden. Her fierce punk look was gone, but its absence had made her prettier and somehow more exotic. We talked for a while and she gave me some acid. And then she was gone. I hope she is well and happy.

That night's venue, the Gloucester Leisure Centre, has since been replaced by GL1 Leisure Centre, a "recreational paradise" offering fun for all the family. Four swimming pools, hair salon, toddler world, two gyms and a spa. Group exercise. It looks fucking horrible. Glass and steel, bunions and athlete's foot. Not that the original was any better, but at least they had gigs. Something for the more dysfunctional family member.

And what a dysfunctional family it is tonight. Wall-to-wall skinheads, hundreds of the bastards, and with them an air of menace so thick you could hang your coat on it. Almost thicker than they are. Never before had I seen so many of them in one place, and rarely since. I arrive at the gig early, one of the first through the doors, so it comes as a gradual realization. There was no sign of them outside the venue, just a handful of punks, and no sign, either, when I went to the bar for the first time, nursing a pint in the hope of doing some minesweeping later. It's only when I come out of the toilet after taking a piss that I notice something is spectacularly wrong, although, in hindsight, the fact that someone had made four attempts – all of them wrong – at drawing a swastika on the toilet wall should have been a clue.

I wander into the main hall and, suddenly, there they are, a small army of shaven-headed nutters. Boots and braces everywhere, all the more sinister when the house lights go down for John Cooper Clarke. They loom out of the darkness like so many zombies in a cheap horror movie. Brains, however, are in desperately short supply, and the question is not *if* they will start trouble but when. The answer, not surprisingly, is almost immediately. Nothing too heavy yet, just some pushing and shoving, flexing of muscles and the inevitable Nazi salutes. Group exercise.

I head back to the bar, thinking it safer to stay in the light, but they've taken over in there, too. Gigantic fuckers with heads like cannonballs and fists like kettlebells, knuckles grazing the floor. Not to mention the smaller specimens, no less dangerous in their keenness to prove themselves. There will be no minesweeping tonight.

One skinhead in particular is especially monstrous, a humongous bone-head who seems to be the result of some terrible genetic experiment. A mutant of such proportions that it's almost impossible not to stare. Not that staring at him is in any way a good idea, but it really is difficult not to. There's this awful compulsion to just gawp at him like some he's some dangerous zoo animal. Except, of course, that someone's made the dreadful mistake of letting this bugger out of his cage. And it's not as if he's some gentle giant. He radiates violent intent, ill will to all men. And women, children, animals, vegetables, inanimate objects. Clearly he is the leader.

A sensible move, at this juncture, would have been to leave. Anywhere but here. Head back to the station and get the last coach back to London. Be on Corrine's doorstep by midnight and in her bed by ten past. But, as has already been well established, common sense has little chance when there's a gig on. So I stay, and try to keep out of the way of skinheads. Which is rather like standing in a thunderstorm and trying not to get wet. And for reasons that still baffle me today, I'm in the middle of the crowd when lightning strikes.

The Banshees have been on stage for maybe half an hour, and the skin-heads are in full swing, Nazi salutes all around and chants of "Sieg Heil" all but drowning out the music. It's fucking terrifying. And there in the middle of the pack, not more than ten feet from me, is the behemoth. Nutter number one. Frothing at the mouth, right arm pumping like a giant piston.

I seem to remember a beard, but I can't be entirely certain. I'd heard somewhere that some of the Banshees road crew also worked for Motörhead, so a beard would make sense. Burly Viking types whose lives were spent on the road and who have grown understandably tired of this shit every night. What I remember, far more vividly, is a baseball bat coming straight through the crowd like a shark's fin. And then a 'thunk', a solid cracking sound, wood on bone, so loud you could hear it above the music.

Nutter number one went down like a sack of shit. There was no confused look, no reeling on his feet, just down and out. Legs gone from underneath him. It was awesome. By which I mean, both shocking and spectacular, inspiring awe. I heard, years later, that the band had to hide the roadie from the police, because he'd fractured the skinhead's skull and almost killed him. From the way he crumpled, it wouldn't surprise me in the least. One minute spewing hatred and violence, then next completely out cold. Game over.

Perhaps not surprisingly, the skinheads seemed to rather lose their enthusiasm after that. With their leader felled in such a brutal fashion they knocked off the stupid chanting and Nazi salutes, and a good number of them scuttled off home, leaving the rest of us to enjoy the gig. I half expected them to lurk around outside the venue, preying on lone punks, but doubtless they were deterred by the police presence and a light drizzle. Even skinheads have the sense not to stand around in the rain waiting to get arrested.

Still, it's not a good idea to be wandering the streets alone at night. If I'm lucky, the train station might be open all night, maybe even an all-night cafe, but who knows what loonies it might attract, what strange moths would be drawn to its flame in the long hours before daylight. My sleeping bag is a blessing when I can use it, essential on cold nights, but it's a curse when there's nowhere to go. It marks me as a stranger in a strange town, a target, and already Gloucester had shown itself to be worryingly hostile. The internet paints a rather different picture of quaint old buildings and a dockyard twinkling by night, a war memorial and a cathedral, but the town centre is still ugly, dirty, and grey. A good place to be on the wrong end of a kicking.

Fortunately, there's a small group of punks, four or five of them, dawdling outside the venue when I leave, and with no better plan, I ask them if they know of any squats around here where I could crash for the night. Without hesitation they say I can stay with them. It would be nice to think that that kind of generosity still exists within the punk community but somehow I doubt it. Too many people will have fucked it up. It would be nicer still if I could remember their names, or even what they looked like. Obviously I could lie, make something up, but somehow that doesn't seem fair. One of them had a small flat in the backstreets of Gloucester, somewhere amongst row upon row of identically drab, brick houses that had once housed single families but are now rented by the room to students. We have to sneak in because he's not allowed guests after dark.

And so we spend a few hours chatting and listening to records. Quietly. It's cramped and floor space is at a premium, but it's warm and dry and the company is good. I'm impressed that someone has their shit together enough to actually *have* a flat, but they seem equally impressed that I'm following the Banshees tour. I may have embellished the facts, what with only managing two gigs so far, but my next stop is Manchester, where they're playing again on Friday. And then the Damned on Saturday. Footloose and fancy-free. Living the life. I probably didn't tell them that I have to go back to work in a factory on Monday. On the Isle of Wight. No need to shatter the illusion. Mine or theirs. I may live with my parents and work at a job I hate, but right now I can lie to myself that I am Jack Kerouac, a nomad wandering wherever the music takes me.

Gloucester, for fuck's sake... Doctor Foster was right about that, at least. No one comes to Gloucester twice if they have a choice in the matter. But for all its faults, I have found a warm welcome here, kindred spirits, even if I may never see them again. At the very least they rescued me from a cold and miserable night, long, long hours of waiting for sunrise. Perhaps I'd have found my way to the motorway and tried to hitch a ride somewhere, but more likely I'd have found myself aimlessly roaming the streets or hiding in a shop doorway. A dark night for the soul. And that's *if* there were no restless skinheads to contend with. Instead, I curl up in my sleeping bag, snug as a bug.

I am woken the next morning by whispered conversation, our host and another male voice. At first I assume their hushed tones are out of politeness, trying not to wake anyone, but then...

"Are you sure it was there?"

"Positive."

"How much?

"Twenty pounds."

This is not good. It doesn't take a pipe-smoking detective to deduce that money has been stolen. It also doesn't take a genius to figure out that as the only unknown I'm the obvious suspect.

CHAPTER TWENTY-TWO

I'LL SPARE YOU the Sherlock Holmes nonsense, wearing a hole in the carpet as we pace back and forth on the living room carpet divulging and dissecting the evidence. It wasn't Colonel Mustard in the library with a candlestick. The two girls have gone and my host is in no doubt that one of them took the money. I am not accused in any way, nor searched, for which I am eternally thankful, not least because out of habit I made a point of telling everyone I had no money, when in fact my cash is hidden in my sock.

It's always wise to lie about such things when you're staying with dodgy guttersnipes, unless you want it to be true. But these are not the thieving scumbags that I'm used to dealing with, unemployable and one step away from being feral, so I felt a pang of guilt in lying, even if it did turn out to be prudent. Admittedly, one of them did turn out to be a thieving scumbag, in many ways worse than those who have nothing and don't know any better. But my point is that I felt safe with them and I lied to them anyway.

Thus, when it's time to leave, I ask directions for the motorway, telling them that I intend to hitchhike, and then double back and head in the opposite direction, towards the train station. It's still raining, and having lost my map I have no idea how to get to Manchester, so the idea of hitching is not appealing. Looking at the map now, it seems that it's only about 140 miles, and quicker to drive than to take the train, an easy hitch – even with the worst of luck – given that I had two days to get there. But my heart just wasn't in it that day, and like Doctor Foster, I never went back to Gloucester again.

On a good day, the train can take anything from two and three quarter hours to nearly four hours, a ludicrous time for such a short journey, little more than forty miles an hour. And that's with today's timetables. For some reason, in 1981 it took all day to get there, crawling along at the speed of smell, frequently stopping at stations that appear to be closed, and forever staring out of the window at the arse end of industrial estates. Perhaps we passed through some beautiful countryside, England's green and pleasant lands, but all I remember is grey and rain and increasing darkness.

It's pitch black by the time I get to Manchester's Piccadilly station, and grim outside, a biblical rain falling. I take one look at the downpour beyond the station exit and decide not to venture any further. Not that I have anywhere to go, but even if I did have somewhere better to spend the night I'd be drenched before I'd taken a few steps. It really is miserable. People making the mad dash to the taxi rank are soaked to the skin in seconds, feet splashing through small rivers as they rush to get home and dry. It can't be much later than maybe six or seven o'clock, maybe earlier, but after grabbing a rather soggy sandwich and a cup of something tepid that claims to be coffee, I find a bench to call my own and settle in for a long night.

I've been there for perhaps an hour when the cops show up, but I'm polite in answering their questions and having checked to see if I'm wanted for anything they leave me in peace. You're not supposed to stay in the station without a valid ticket, but it would take a truly heartless bastard to kick someone out on a night like this. Today I find entire websites dedicated to the storm, a nationwide event that turned day into night and made front page headlines. By all accounts 113mm of rain fell on Manchester. Not that I have any real idea what that means, but some 35mm fell on London, causing widespread flooding, and in Epsom no less than 16 buildings were struck by lightning. Manchester's wet at the best of times, but it was truly torrential that night.

I manage to doze off for an hour or so and then wander the lonely platforms for a while to stretch my legs, but there's nothing much else to do but listen to the relentless drum solo on the roof of the station. The place has been modernised in recent years, glass and steel and fancy-looking eateries replacing dirty Victorian brick, and doubtless there is a book store or someplace else to kill time, but all I could do that night was wait.

The worst of the storm passes sometime in the small hours and by morning it's just grey and damp rather than apocalyptic. To save carrying it around all day and attracting unwanted attention, I put my sleeping bag in a station locker – something I would imagine no longer exists due to terrorism – and venture out to explore the city. I turn right out of the station, simply because it looks better than turning left, and 15 minutes later find myself wandering outside the Arndale, a vast shopping centre with all the appeal of a genital wart.

The Arndale was constructed in phases, between 1972 and 1979, so would have been quite new in 1981, but even then it was a concrete carbuncle. In his book, *Notes From A Small Island*, Bill Bryson points out that it must be quite nice, in a place as rainy as Manchester, to have a place to do one's shopping indoors, but he then describes the place, quite accurately, as 'looking like the world's largest gents' lavatory'. In 1996, it was vastly improved by a 3,330lb IRA bomb that could be heard 15 miles away and left a 50ft crater.

Indeed, much of the city seems to have been improved by the bomb, forcing mass regeneration and economic growth, and when I returned in 2003 I was surprised to find such modernisation. Mean-looking streets were now well-lit and clean, and my last visit in 2015 suggested that it had stayed that way. Admittedly, standing outside a bar for a few minutes to have a cigarette also suggested that it was still a good place to get harassed by passing pissheads, but at least it *looked* nicer. It was still raining though.

But I digress. In 1981 it was a dump and a dangerous one at that. To kill some time and stay out of the rain I decide to take a look around the Arndale, but I'm stopped on my way in by a little old lady.

"I wouldn't go in there if I was you, love," she warns. "You'll get stabbed."

Being young and foolish – not to mention cold and damp – I ignore her advice and go for a wander around the shops. I vaguely remember a record store, but mostly it seems to be Indian clothing shops, Boots, Marks and Spencer, electrical goods, travel agent's… One of the clothing shops has a decent selection of bootleg T-shirts, so I get myself an Exploited shirt, unaware at the time that the bands don't see any of the money. Then again, I've still got that shirt, so obviously it wasn't bad quality.

Eventually enough time passes that the box office for tonight's venue will be close to opening, so I head back to the train station to retrieve my sleeping bag and then walk the mile or so to the Apollo Theatre on Stockton Road. Built in 1938, it's an impressive, Grade II listed building with a glazed white terracotta facade made all the more imposing by its drab surroundings. Since the '60s it's hosted everyone from the Beatles and the Rolling Stones to, well, just about every big band you can name.

Having said that, it is – or was – a disappointing venue in which to see bands; the bouncers were surly and, worse still, it was seated, with seating rigorously enforced by said bouncers, so you had to stay put. Dancing was frowned upon. I've been back since, many times over the years, and they've taken the seats out, which is a drastic improvement, but those first impressions have never left. There's something quite lonely about going to a show on your own if you're not allowed to mingle outside the bar or the foyer, more so because you're so much less likely to make friends with anyone, or in this case find a place to stay after the show.

Not that it's a bad show by any means, and it's a welcome surprise that the place isn't full of skinheads, perhaps because they know they can't cause any trouble here. Remarkably, I've found a setlist from the show online, which is pretty much as I remember it – opening with *Israel* and *Halloween* – but even without the reminder I can vividly recall *Night Shift* being spectacular. And then – having headed to the cloakroom to get my sleeping bag before the encore – the mad dash back inside to hear a rare airing of *Love In A Void*. Bouncers be damned, we danced to that one.

The thought of spending another night in the train station is quite dreadful, as is the prospect of walking that long mile after dark, but once again I get lucky, this time in meeting a couple of local punks, Jesus and Toothpaste, who play for a band called Varicose Veins. They're outside the venue handing out flyers for their latest EP, which features such 'classics' as *Grandma's Got VD* and *Maggie Thatcher's Got Piles*, the sleeve depicting a crude cut-and-paste collage of Prince Charles shagging Princess Diana, and they kindly offer me a place to stay. In doing so, they undoubtedly saved me from a night of hell.

In that strange way that so often happens after gigs, 3,500 Banshees fans suddenly vanish, all heading home in different directions, and we find ourselves on an otherwise empty bus, which takes us to some sort of depot, also empty but for a few drivers ending their shifts. Or so it seems. It's about fifteen minutes until our next bus, but rather than just walk across the depot to the other stop, Toothpaste and I wait as Jesus nervously goes on ahead to check things out, sneaking along behind billboards and bus shelters, like a cat in the night. He returns with bad news.

"Perry Boys," he whispers.

I have no idea what Perry Boys are – evidently a local gang who dress themselves in Fred Perry clothing – but the fact that Jesus and Toothpaste are so jumpy about them tells me all I need to know. There are seven of them, three of us, and in order to get to our stop we have to cross about 100 yards of well-lit ground without being seen. Apparently this is a regular occurrence and there is a knack to it.

Jesus peeks his head around the corner again. The Perry Boys are still there. Fourteen minutes to go. Or maybe ten. Buses are unreliable. Sometimes they turn up on time, sometimes early, sometimes late. The trick, I'm told, is to wait until the bus pulls in, then leg it full pelt across the depot just as the doors are opening. Run too soon and you risk getting caught before you can get on the bus, run too late and it will fuck off without you.

And so begins the longest ten or fifteen minutes in history. We wait. Jesus pokes his head around the corner. The Perry Boys are still there and the bus isn't. Then we wait some more, the process repeated every few minutes, each peek increasing the risk of being spotted but essential – since we can't see the bus stop – so we don't miss the damn bus. The alternative is a very long walk, peppered with mad dashes to safety as we make our way through various sketchy neighbourhoods that are littered with numerous other gangs. Imagine the 1979 movie *The Warriors,* but with just three rather reluctant warriors.

At long last, the bus shows up and we run. I'll say one thing, Jesus and Toothpaste have their timing down to perfection. The Perry Boys look around, clearly taken off guard, but they don't have time to react, let alone give chase. We're home and dry. Well, someone's home at least, and only slightly damp.

CHAPTER TWENTY-THREE

THERE WERE A lot of marches in the '80s. March against apartheid. March for jobs. March against racism. Gay rights. Women's rights. Troops out of Ireland. Save the whales. You name it, there was a march for or against it. I'm still not entirely convinced that they achieved anything other than giving the police an opportunity to photograph the ringleaders and beat the snot of out people they didn't like, but I'd go on them anyway and often we were rewarded with a free festival in whatever park we'd marched to.

It seemed like every other week there was a march for nuclear disarmament – which definitely achieved bugger all, since the UK still has nuclear weapons – and in Manchester that Saturday it was the Northern March Against Missiles, featuring the Damned, Hawkwind, the ubiquitous John Cooper Clarke, local band the Freshies, Ronnie Lane – whose name was misspelled on the flyers – a local reggae band called Harlem Spirit – also misspelled – and a laser show.

I must confess I don't recall doing any actual marching that day, but I don't remember why. I stayed with Jesus the previous night, who lived, I think, with his parents in a council house, but I may be wrong, and perhaps they lived a long way from Strangeways, the starting point of the march. Certainly, I didn't stay with Toothpaste, because he was black. Well, not *because* he was black, obviously, but because I would have remembered staying with a black family as something I'd never done before, since the Isle of Wight is not exactly racially integrated. Let's be clear, I liked

Toothpaste a great deal and racism is fucking stupid. Anyway, the march started at 11am, so maybe we overslept. Or, quite likely, we just couldn't be arsed to walk that far in the pissing rain. Either way, we met with Toothpaste in the morning, and what I do vividly recall is walking down Princess Road to get to Alexander Park in Moss Side, where the festival was being held.

Less than a month earlier Moss Side had been the centre of savage rioting, which according to The Hytner Report, started on the morning of July 8th when a brick was thrown through a pawn shop window. Minutes later, shop windows on Princess Road were smashed and the first petrol bombs were thrown. By nightfall over 1,000 'youths' – reportedly led by a nine-year-old boy – attacked Moss Side police station, breaking all the windows and setting vehicles on fire in what was later described as 'a spontaneous eruption of hatred'. One officer was said to have been shot in the leg with a crossbow, and for an hour or more there was virtually no police presence as shops and homes went up in flames.

Like the rioting all over the UK that summer, the reasons are many and obvious – racial tension, police brutality, massive unemployment – and the results were devastating. But perhaps none more so than in Manchester. In Brixton, or at least the part I saw, there were no visible scars, but in Manchester it seemed as if an entire neighbourhood had been burned to the ground, nothing left but blackened, charred remains. It was a sobering sight.

We arrive at the festival site sometime in the afternoon and the rain subsides, although the skies are still dishwater grey. Police presence is low-key to say the least and people are openly smoking joints, the 35,000 strong crowd a healthy mixture of all kinds, hippies, punks, Rastas, students and the like. I now discover that when it was opened to the public in 1870, the purpose of Alexander Park was to 'deter the working men of Manchester from the alehouses', which is ironic since we were all getting pissed on cheap cider. But then, we weren't really working.

I can't pretend to recall much about the bands. The reggae band played some reggae, the Freshies played pop punk that I didn't really enjoy, John Cooper Clarke did *Evidently Chickentown* and some other stuff that I wasn't paying attention to. Hawkwind didn't show up. Sometime later in the day I ran into Dragon Tim and a guy called Taff with three punk girls, all of them having travelled up from London, so we hung out, chatting and drinking and mostly just waiting for the Damned to come on. Jesus and Toothpaste had wandered off to the front, but I was in good company and excited, as always, to see one of my favourite bands. To this day I can't recommend the Damned enough.

But somehow, for reasons that were never entirely clear, the atmosphere had soured before they came on. I later heard that the hippies were disgruntled that Hawkwind never showed up, and started throwing bottles at the punks from behind the stage. I also heard – which sounds more likely – that the bouncers were starting trouble. Maybe people were just pissed off that there was no laser show. Whatever the case, the mood had turned dark and it became obvious that violence was imminent.

Again, thanks to some poking about on the internet, I've managed to find a setlist from the show – kicking off with *Wait For The Blackout, Lively Arts*, and *I Just Can't Be Happy Today* – but even without it I remember that it was around the aptly named *Smash It Up* that the fighting started, all of it focused by the barrier at the front of the stage. Bottles and fists came from both sides of the fence, with Captain Sensible batting cans and bottles away with a handy cricket bat-shaped guitar. Several times the band stop playing and appeal for calm, but the fighting continues until the end of the set.

When they're done playing we head out of the park, Tim, Taff, the girls and I, and ask directions for the Mayflower club on Birch Street, where the Damned are doing another show, this one a benefit for the Greater Manchester Play Recourse Unit, whatever that might be. I can't find Jesus or Toothpaste, which would have been handy since they know the area, but there are enough local punks heading in that direction, so we follow them. It turns out to be an hour-long walk, back past all the burned-out buildings and through some seriously sketchy parts of town where the only thing that stops us getting attacked is safety in numbers. Even then, there are moments when I'm not entirely sure we're going to get there in one piece. With every step it is made clear that we are deep in enemy territory.

The Mayflower club, when we finally get there, turns out to be in an equally dubious neighbourhood, alone in what quite frankly looks like wasteland. It's long gone now, apparently burned down in 1984 and demolished in 1985, which is a great shame, because for all its faults the 1,100 capacity venue had a remarkable history. Opened in 1915 as the Corona Picture Theatre, it was converted into a dance hall in the 1950s and remained a popular venue until its demise. By all accounts, the Beatles played there and signed their names on the dressing room walls, and in the '70s it saw the likes of Joy Division, Wire, Buzzcocks, the Fall and more, although there are many stories of Teddy Boys from the nearby Ardwick and West Gorton estates kicking the shit of punks on their way home.

One website suggests that it had fallen into dereliction by 1980, which explains why it was such a shithole in 1981, but it was still the site of some phenomenal punk shows – Discharge, GBH, Dead Kennedys, Exploited, Crass and more – and even then it didn't take too much imagination to see its former grandeur. It had the look of a castle at the front, with a huge arched doorway and tall turrets on either side, and should probably have been a listed building. There's some sort of office block there now and a Travelodge, which is strange because there seems to be no possible reason to stay there.

As you'd imagine, the place was absolutely packed, many people sharing their adventures from that afternoon's skirmish. When Jesus shows up he is still bleeding quite heavily from a head wound having been on the wrong side of a kicking, and another friend has a lump on his head the size of a golf ball from getting hit with a bottle. It seems like pretty much everyone has a mad tale to tell, but remarkably there are no serious injuries. A few cuts and scrapes, a black eye here and there, but no missing teeth or broken bones. It could have been a lot worse.

And so we set about getting pissed – or more pissed – until the Damned come on, which is probably why I don't remember an opening band. It's an 18 and over show, but as usual no one has bothered to check IDs. Come to think of it, I'm not even sure I had ID since it wasn't a legal requirement in those days, not to mention being largely pointless as they didn't have photos on them. It's not like the cops would have been in any hurry to show up to a place like this, and I'm guessing that health inspectors were rather less thick on the ground than the beer we were standing in.

The Damned, it should go without saying, were fantastic again. I managed to find a setlist for that evening's show, too, but somehow failed to bookmark it and have just wasted several hours trying to find it again. Suffice to say, it was completely different from the afternoon set, although no less chaotic. I've seen them literally hundreds of times over the years and rarely do they put on a bad performance. And they really don't get enough credit for it. The Sex Pistols may have changed everything, but they seem to have been trying to change it back ever since. The Clash got boring about halfway through *London Calling*. But the Damned have always had something special about them. With the exception of Motörhead I've seen them more than any other band. And it was only two quid to get in.

For some reason they went on late that night, maybe midnight, so we hang around after the show, Tim, Taff, the punk girls and I, trying to figure out where to go. Jesus has gone off to get his head looked at and couldn't be expected to put us all up anyway. The train station is half an hour away, a scary walk since there are no buses, and there won't be any trains until morning. The club empties while we're standing around, and Rat Scabies comes out for a chat, which is cool, but leaves us no closer to having a plan. I'm just thankful not to be facing the night alone.

Eventually the staff make it apparent that they're going to be locking up soon and they'd rather like us to go away. The band's gear is packed up and no doubt already halfway down the motorway, Scabies bids us farewell – or words to that effect – and we make our way to the exit. Pretty much everyone has gone.

Which is when we realise that we've got a serious problem.

We get to the big, glass-fronted door, lights going off in the club behind us, and there on the other side of the road, illuminated by street lights, we can see about twenty or so of our friends the Perry Boys staring back at us. There is no bus stop across the street, but the fact that they are carrying baseball bats suggests that they're not waiting for a bus. They're waiting for us.

CHAPTER TWENTY-FOUR

I HAVE, OVER the years, spent countless bitterly cold nights sleeping rough after gigs. Far more than I care to remember. Of course, there were tricks to staying out of the cold, even sleeping under recently parked cars to get some heat, but sometimes there was simply no way to keep warm. Minutes pass like hours and even daylight brings no relief until you can get off the streets. Still, it can take hours more before you stop shivering. It really is miserable, and about as far removed from the romantic notion of sleeping under the stars as it's possible to get. And few of those nights were as wretched as the one that followed the Damned's show in Manchester.

By no small miracle we are saved from a savage beating at the hands – feet and baseball bats – of the Perry Boys by one of the last people to leave the venue, a man who happened to have a transit van in which to sneak us all out the back way. I later learned that Perry Boys, a precursor to soccer casuals who later became card-carrying gangsters, were also known for carrying knives, so he probably saved us from getting stabbed. For which I will be eternally grateful, although it has to be said that a night or two in hospital began, in those long, long hours, to seem like a luxury compared to what we went through.

Maybe there was nowhere safe in the city to drop us off, or maybe he thought we'd be able to get a ride back to London, but for whatever reason, the man dropped the six of us, Tim, Taff, the three girls and I, on some remote stretch of motorway outside Manchester. I have no idea where; it was dark and there were no signs. There was also no other traffic. Not a soul in sight, and no sign, even in the far distance, of any civilisation. We were in the middle of fucking nowhere.

Worse still, a foul wind picked up, cutting us to the bone, and there was no shelter, except, up ahead, a motorway flyover, which at least offered some protection if it started raining again. And so we climbed the short, steep incline to find that the ground beneath the flyover was made up entirely of filthy gravel and small, sharp rocks, perhaps undisturbed since the flyover was first constructed. Certainly, there were no empty beer cans or old socks, no graffiti to suggest that anyone else had been here. And why would they? A shop doorway would offer more comfort. Indeed, the flyover seemed to act as some sort of wind tunnel, howling like a stray dog, a mournful cry to echo our moods.

But still, I was better equipped than the others, Tim and Taff in holey jeans and leather jackets, the girls wearing miniskirts and fishnets, while I had the luxury of a sleeping bag. It's not long before one of the girls asks if she can share it with me, and though I'm reluctant at first because I was under the impression that she was Tim's girlfriend, he doesn't seem to be bothered. No sense in all of us freezing to death, so we spend the night pressed together for warmth, still shivering like we've got Parkinson's disease, but vastly more comfortable than the others. I can only imagine what they went through. As it was, we probably slept for no more than an hour.

We are up with the first grey light of dawn, grimy and aching with cold, somehow still alive, but still very much in the middle of nowhere. From the top of a grass bank, it's possible to see another stretch of motorway which looks to have more traffic, but it's impossible to tell where it goes. Anywhere but here would be a good start.

Unfortunately, any idiot can see that we're not going to get a ride unless we split up. Aside from the obvious point that few cars will have enough room for six extra passengers, there is also the regrettable fact that we look rather like we've spent the night sleeping under a bridge. On top of which, Tim's carefully cultivated look of menace, while being most useful for scaring boneheads, is equally likely to frighten the crap out of potential Good Samaritans who might be otherwise inclined to pick us up. Clearly our best chance is to split up into couples, so that's exactly what we don't do.

With the other motorway looking like a better bet, the others decide to head that way across a field, while I, with my vastly superior knowledge of hitching, decide to stick with this route and go it alone. Sure, there's less traffic here and I'll have to walk a while to find a better place for cars to pull over, but, let's face it, they're never going to get a ride. Not in a month of Sundays. I wish them the best of luck and we go our separate ways. Suckers.

It is with some astonishment, then, that I watch from across the field as my friends are picked up almost immediately, all piling into the back of a truck, which I later found out took them all the way to London. Somewhat dejected, I keep walking. And walking. And walking some more. It starts to rain.

I must have walked maybe three miles before the sun decides to make a casual appearance, but for all its tardiness it promises another hot day and my spirits lift. I still have no idea where I am or where I'm going, but the traffic has increased and with it my chances of getting a ride, and at least I'm not cold anymore. Surely my luck must change.

And it does. At long last a car pulls over. A police car.

Two cops get out and I give them my brightest smile, genuinely pleased to see them, and foolishly thinking they might be of some assistance. If nothing else they'll be able to tell me if I'm going in the right direction. But, alas, it becomes immediately clear that these are not your friendly local bobbies. They search me by the side of the road and take down my details, running a background check to make sure I have no outstanding warrants. And then they arrest me for walking on a motorway, which contravenes section blah of the road traffic act. I explain that I had no choice and fully intend not to do so just as soon as I possibly can, but they are utterly humourless cunts, immune to my politeness and obviously intent on being as unpleasant as possible. It matters not that I wasn't actually walking on the motorway but on a grass bank, staying out of harm until I could find somewhere to hitch from. It matters not that I am lost and alone. They bundle me into the back of the car and we drive in silence.

Even then, some naive part of my brain thought that they'd take me, if not to a police station, then perhaps to somewhere I might stand some chance of getting a ride. But no. Instead, I am taken to the nearest junction, a remote roundabout with signs for places I don't recognise, villages

I've never heard of, and with stern warnings of what will happen if I break the law again, they leave me there.

It is entirely possible that no one has ever tried hitching from this godforsaken junction before, or since. Certainly, there is no traffic, not a single passing car for at least an hour, and afraid that I'll accidentally stray onto a motorway if I start walking, I stay put and wait. And wait. And wait some more. Slowly, I come to the realization that I will have to live here.

When all hope is finally gone, a lone car, the only car I've seen for hours, comes my way. Against all possible odds the driver pulls in to the grass verge. A middle-aged man, slightly chubby and balding but otherwise nondescript. He has the look of an accountant or maybe a teacher. Geography.

"Where are you going?" he asks.

"Anywhere that's not here."

We're about ten minutes into our journey when he starts telling me about his loveless marriage and how his wife doesn't understand him, how lonely he is. Sadly, it's not an unfamiliar story. A lot of people who pick up hitchhikers are lonely, just looking for some company. The geography teacher, however, is looking for something rather more than company, as I discover a few minutes later when he puts his hand on my knee.

"Um, I'm not really, uh…" I bluster, sharply aware that we're doing 60 miles an hour and I can't just jump out of the car.

I'm pleased that he keeps his eyes on the road, but not so overjoyed that he keeps his hand on my knee.

"I've read all about punk rockers," he tells me. "Orgies and all sorts."

Quite where he's read this is anyone's guess. Even the most salacious so-called newspapers, *The Sun* and *News of the World,* tend, when they're not encouraging people to beat punks to death for the good of humanity, to stick mostly to the drugs and violence angle. The sick world of punk star Sid. Not that I'm in the habit of reading such rags, but I don't remember any mention of orgies.

Granted, I would later find out that such reports were not entirely untrue, but at such a tender age I had no clue. My first thought was that there probably weren't enough punks on the Isle of Wight to even manage an orgy without busing a few in from the mainland. Well, perhaps not my *first* thought, which was more along the lines of 'how the fuck do I get out of this situation?' But it certainly came to mind. What if someone's mum walked in?

Much to my dismay, I would also discover, long after the fact, that I had inadvertently been advertising my sexual preferences and in my naïvety sending out quite the wrong signals. I always wondered why I got hit on by so many gay men, but it turned out that by wearing a red handkerchief in my back pocket – because I was young and copying the Sex Pistols – I was in fact telling the gay world that I was a submissive who enjoyed fisting. It could have been worse, I suppose, the handkerchief could have been brown, but it did lead to an extraordinary amount of lifts from disappointed men of all ages.

Luckily, my tender age saves us both from further embarrassment. The age of consent is – or was in 1981 – 21 and I'm obviously younger than that, a point I make clear when I lie and tell the amorous driver that I have to go to school tomorrow. He couldn't have moved his hand any faster if my knee was on fire.

We drive in silence. No more talk of orgies or unhappy marriages. At last we pass a sign: Liverpool 26 Miles. Which means I've been going in the wrong direction all morning, west when I should have been going south. By strange coincidence, I seem to remember that Siouxsie and the Banshees are playing in Liverpool tonight, but as tempting as it might be to go and see them I have work in the morning and I'm still a long way from home.

Perhaps it crossed my mind that I wasn't going to make it anyway – fuck work, just keep going – but any doubt is taken away when my driver decides he's taken me as far as he's willing to go. It's not the first time that my inadvertent false advertising has led to an abrupt end of my journey, but in this case maybe I should be thankful. Especially since I'd got the dates wrong and the Banshees were in Newcastle. He drops me off within sight of a town and I have no choice but to walk. Obviously, I can't walk to Liverpool nor hitch there since this quiet little hamlet seems all but empty, but against all odds there is a train station, just one platform, and the first train out of here is going to London.

I am going home.

CHAPTER TWENTY-FIVE

YARMOUTH HAS A quaint little harbour and a rich history that dates back hundreds of years, the town itself first documented in records of the Danegeld tax of 991. And no, that's not missing a 1. Apparently the tax was to pay off Viking raiding parties, which, unless you count the annual carnival, is probably the last party this place ever saw. Christ, it's dull.

Of course, I get it, dull is good. When the nearest thing to a headline is 'Man Stung By Wasp' or a well-mannered protest about parking fees, you can be pretty sure that you'll live a long and uneventful life. And even if you don't, it will certainly fucking feel like it.

But Yarmouth, for me, holds rather mixed memories in that it was either my escape from or my return to the Isle of Wight on the Wightlink car ferry, which seems to dwarf the harbour with its arrival and departure every hour. On weekdays, when there was a gig on in Southampton, I'd get back around eight o'clock in the morning, after sleeping rough the night before, just in time to walk to work and clock in at nine. Obviously, leaving was always better than coming back, but either way the ferry crossing offered time for reflection and a strange sense of longing. Mostly longing not to be on the Isle of Wight.

Somehow I had managed, that day, to get from an obscure train station on the outskirts of Liverpool to London, then on to Southampton and Lymington in time to get the last ferry, and all I had to deal with now was a three mile walk home. It was dark, but it had the decency not to rain.

There was no one in when I got back, no warm welcome – not that I expected one – and no one to talk to, not that there was anything to say. Hey, mum, guess what I did? I was already a disgrace to the family, an irredeemable let-down, and it wasn't as if anything I had done over the past weeks would change that. Particularly since there would be a summons arriving in the post for my terrible crime of walking on the motorway. I'd be lucky not to make the local papers: Local Youth In Motorway Madness!

Actually, that's not entirely true: In 1981 there was a massive cannabis bust on the Isle of Wight, which rather eclipsed my nefarious deeds, and there were frequent stories of violent assaults, nasty bastards glassing people in pubs. Indeed, if you're looking for headlines, in 1999 police raided a house in Cowes and found no less than 50 million in counterfeit banknotes, the crime ring apparently responsible for around two thirds of the UK's fake currency. But most of the time it was stuff like revised bus timetables, inclement weather, charity bingo, and occasional road accidents. I'm looking at it now and the top story is about a man headbutting a door, followed by another story about someone winning car dealer of the year.

Anyway, I had a bath and went to bed, then got up the next morning and walked to work at the factory. 55 pence an hour for eight hours. Walk home in the rain. Repeat until Friday, when the highlight of the week is picking up *Sounds* magazine and scouring the gig guide. The Banshees are still on tour, Aberdeen in Scotland, this being when bands did proper UK tours. I would be spending the weekend in my room listening to records, or maybe walking aimlessly around a town where sitting in a bus shelter passed for entertainment. So very tired of being a cuckoo, I was more than ready to fly away. Anywhere but here.

A small part of me now understands the appeal of a place that never changes, where you can go on Google Street View so many years later and still see a place where everything is familiar. The same pubs and churches, the same petrol station, the same village green. Every day the same. It's nice until you reach your teens, comforting, and some people never leave, but for me it was a prison.

Admittedly, there have been little changes here and there, drastic for the island. There's kebab shops now, Chinese restaurants, even tattoo parlours. And let's not forget the festival, rekindled in 2002 after 32 years.

It's never going to be as legendary as Hendrix, The Who, and The Doors playing to a quarter of a million hippies, but they've had some more than decent line-ups including Bowie, the Damned, Sex Pistols, The Prodigy, Foo Fighters, and more.

But for the most part the Island lives in its own tiny bubble, twinned with Neverland, forever frozen in time. Which is not always as delightful as it sounds if that time was somewhere between 1800 and 1945. The last time I was there, my wife and I took a walk around Victoria Arcade in Ryde, a small shopping centre that opened in 1836. We found, amongst the knick-knacks and book stores, a shop that sold, along with its World War Two memorabilia, golliwogs and portraits of Hitler. Anywhere else it would have been burned down, but here it was perfectly normal.

But as much as I hated the Isle of Wight, there is every possibility that I wouldn't have fitted in anywhere else, always the strange kid, the loner. My younger brothers describe their childhoods as idyllic and I can see why, but only from a distance. At the time, I think I resented them for it, for fitting in. My stepfather was a decent enough man, but I hated him because he wasn't my dad. I was just the right age to be devastated by my parents' divorce. It didn't help that I was sexually assaulted by a local council member and never told anyone.

Punk rock came along at just the right time. A month into my teens the Sex Pistols released *God Save The Queen* and, already obsessed with music, I was completely hooked. Puberty and punk rock. It spoke to me in ways that, perhaps, can only be fully understood from the same vantage point. I was already questioning all the bullshit and hypocrisy we were being force-fed in school, the great British Empire, religion, learning absolutely nothing that would ever be useful. I hated being at school, hated being at home, and then, having left school at sixteen with no qualifications, hated work. Me and thousands of others.

We were too young to ride the first wave of punk, but the second wave was ours. At thirteen years old I had to look up anarchy in the dictionary, but by fourteen I was in my own band. And while there is no doubt that the Pistols opened the door, they were gone in the blink of an eye, already a parody. Sidney was dead. Rotten was in Jamaica with Richard Branson. Jones and Cook were in Rio making rubbish singles with Ronnie Biggs.

Instead we had the Damned, Discharge, Killing Joke, Crass, the Exploited, Cockney Rejects, Dead Kennedys, Stiff Little Fingers, Angelic Upstarts, the Ruts, UK Subs, 999, and so many more. And I loved them all.

But I digress. We're back in the factory, nine-to-five. No prospects. No future for you. Home is just somewhere I sleep. I should have been grateful that I wasn't cold or hungry, wasn't being beaten, but at the same time if I'd been able to open my mouth without being criticised… Yeah, cry me a river. It could have been a lot worse, but it could have been a lot better. We've given up on you, I was told.

At the end of August I went to see the Banshees again. Southampton Gaumont on their never-ending *Juju* tour. Remarkably, John McGeoch came and sat with me for a while before the show. He'd seen me in the crowd, recognised my face. Fuck knows how. I think he thought I was a runaway and he wanted to make sure I was okay. He was a wonderful person.

"Did you get in alright?"

"Um, yeah, I bought a ticket."

He looks mildly surprised. Puts me on the guest list for the remainder of the tour. But summer is gone and it's a Monday night. The metal-pressing machine hits me in the face when I nod off at work the next day. I'm saving as best I can to leave. Anywhere but here. Doubtless every shitty town was the same. In October the Exploited were on *Top Of The Pops* doing *Dead Cities.*

But still there are gigs to keep me sane, the Stranglers at the Gaumont, the Damned at the Gaumont, and between them another trip to London for the nightmare that was the inappropriately named Woodstock Revisited all-dayer at the Rainbow with, among others, Angelic Upstarts, Vice Squad, Anti Pasti, and a couple of thousand skinheads. The review in *Sounds* said that punk was dead, and it was certainly very ill that night, but we had nothing else. A night of bad drugs and terrible violence. Zombie punks shuffling out of the darkness, off their faces on Tuinal and glue. Skinheads kicking the shit out of everyone; first the punks, then the bouncers, and then each other.

All the time I was a ghost at home. Barely there. Barely talking. I knew the end was coming.

It was early evening when my stepfather pulled me aside in the kitchen. He was a man of very few words, but he didn't need many.

"I think it's time you were moving on, don't you?"

I don't know where he expected me to go. I wasn't legally old enough to rent a place to live and certainly not equipped to do so, but I didn't argue. I wanted to leave as much as he wanted me gone. He gave me fifty pounds.

And so I worked out my two weeks' notice at the factory. I don't know why.

I packed my bags on Saturday, just a few possessions. My sleeping bag and a few records. It was dark when I left that afternoon, winter dark. My mother watched me go, but I didn't look back. There was no bus, so I started walking. Stuck my thumb out in the hope of hitching a ride. I had no idea where I was going. London. Anywhere but here.

Printed in Great Britain
by Amazon